Happy Birthday, Hollywood!
One Hundred Years of Magic
1887-1987

Published by
THE MOTION PICTURE AND TELEVISION FUND
Hollywood, California

Text compiled by Michael Webb

Edited by Peter B. Wert and Robert A. Oettinger

Photo Editor: Marc Wanamaker/The Bison Archives

Graphic Design: Jack Schnyder, Advertising and Design Inc.
Jack Schnyder, Laura Hilstrom, and Susan Alinsangan

Printed in Japan
Second Edition
ISBN 0-9618040-0-9

Table of Contents

Foreword

The Motion Picture and Television Fund is a unique institution in the United States and quite probably in the world. Since 1921, when pioneers of the fledgling film industry recognized the need to establish a means for helping its members in times of economic trouble, psychological and emotional distress and social need, the Fund has met its simple, yet challenging promise: "We take care of our own." It gives me great pleasure to be a part of an industry that combines the heart and muscle to care for its own people.

As our industry expanded, so did the needs of its workers and the Motion Picture and Television Fund grew along with its constituency. In 1940, Motion Picture Relief Fund (as we were then known) President Jean Hersholt purchased 48 acres, at $850 per acre, in Woodland Hills for the future site of the Country House and Hospital. Groundbreaking ceremonies were held the following year and the Motion Picture Country House, Y. Frank Freeman Library and Louis B. Mayer Dining Room were dedicated in 1942. Several years later, the Motion Picture Country Hospital was constructed and the Hollywood Health Care Clinic opened its doors in 1951. With the emergence of television, the Fund expanded its scope to accommodate members of this new industry and changed its name to the Motion Picture and Television Fund.

By the early 1980's, the comprehensive health care, social welfare, financial and retirement programs and facilities provided by the Fund were so successful, waiting periods of up to four years had developed for admission to the Woodland Hills campus. In 1985, the Board of Trustees of the Fund launched a $50 million Capital Campaign to double the capacity of the Country House and Hospital, from 300 to 600 and to renovate and modernize other facilities. Proceeds from the sale of this book are benefitting the Capital Campaign.

The services provided by the Motion Picture and Television Fund are not reserved solely for actors. Every year, approximately 20,000 people benefit from one or more of the Fund's services and the vast majority of them work behind the cameras...as producers, directors, writers, electricians, grips, even the security guards. I have had the pleasure of visiting friends at the Country House and Hospital and have always been impressed with the quality of care and the genuine feelings of concern that I have seen.

Hollywood knows no geographic boundaries and I believe that each of us is influenced at least in some way by the film industry. This book captures the rich history of this world community and I can think of no more fitting beneficiary of this work than the industry's charity for its own people, the Motion Picture and Television Fund.

Clint Eastwood

Introduction

A centennial is a mark of accomplishment: failures don't stay the course. A hundred years ago, Hollywood was laid out as a new community. Its first notable achievement was to survive: most of the new towns that were ballyhooed in the land boom of 1887 vanished from the map. Its second coup was to lure a fledgling industry and become the world capital of motion pictures.

As Harvey Wilcox was registering the subdivision of Hollywood, pioneers on the far side of the continent and in Europe were inventing the movies, drawing on a century of experiments, and the latest advances in optics and photography. Within a year of the first public demonstration, in Paris, in December 1895, the movies had become the first vehicle of mass entertainment, produced and shown around the world. Few inventions have moved from the laboratory to the market place with such rapidity, or been received with such overwhelming acclaim.

Within twenty years, the movies had gone West, transforming a community of sedate former mid-Westerners into a factory town. Hollywood became a household word in every land, shorthand for a product and for the American dream—fast-paced, star-studded, optimistic and larger than life. Sixty years on, Federico Fellini received the homage of his American admirers at Lincoln Center, and recalled the impact of that dream:

"In the small movie house of my village—with two hundred seats and five hundred standing room—I discovered through your films that there existed another way of life, that a country existed of wide-open spaces, of fantastic cities which were like a cross between Babylon and Mars. Perhaps, thinking about it now, the stories were simplistic. However, it was nice to think that despite the conflicts and the pitfalls there was always a happy ending. It was especially wonderful to know that a country existed where people were free, rich and happy, dancing on the roofs of the skyscrapers, and where even a humble tramp could become President. Perhaps even then it wasn't really like this. However, I believe that I owe to those flickering shadows from America my decision to express myself through film."

In Europe, the movies had enjoyed respect from the start; in America they were derided by artists and denounced by moralists. Overshadowed by the legitimate theater in the big cities, they were created by poor immigrants for working-class audiences and shown in spartan theaters. It was from these humble beginnings that Adolph Zukor and William Fox, Samuel Goldwyn and Louis B. Mayer, Marcus Loew and Carl Laemmle—all refugees from Eastern Europe, and such familiar names as DeMille, Lasky and Griffith, created an empire on the far shore of the continent. They succeeded because they were outsiders, unconstrained by tradition. They had an instinctive grasp of audience taste, and the drive to reach far beyond. The movies' rough childhood was a source of strength: it gave them the common touch. For every spectator who applauded Sarah Bernhardt, a thousand laughed at Charlie Chaplin, or fell in love with Mary Pickford.

Hollywood offered these empire builders the territory they needed for expansion. Its prime assets were light, locations, land and labor. The first pioneers were birds of passage, in flight from New York and Chicago winters. They discovered they could shoot outdoors, without harsh klieg lights, and they eagerly exploited the varied locations of ocean and desert, mountain and Mission.

Cheap land and unorganized labor encouraged them to establish studios. At first, these comprised of little more than a wooden stage, with muslin canopies to diffuse the sun, and a cottage for administration and dressing rooms. Cecil B. De Mille made his first picture in a rented horse barn.

Out West, the movies were reborn. A cottage industry became a production line; talent was put under contract and concentrated within high-walled compounds. Stars and studios flourished in tandem, making motion pictures hugely profitable, and increasingly artistic. They also became more polished and respectable in order to win and hold the middle-class audience. The earliest movies were documentaries of every-day events: workers leaving a factory, a mother feeding her baby. The first stars intensified commonplace occurrences: Chaplin as an immigrant fresh off the boat, unable to pay for his dinner, pursued by a cop, mirrored the first-hand experiences of his audience. Hollywood elaborated on the experience, creating fantasies that were prefaced, "What if...?"

A few big companies dominated, and though ultimate power rested with their head offices in New York, Hollywood was so far away—physically and psychologically—and production became so complex, that studio moguls exercised almost unlimited authority within their domains. Thus the outsiders found themselves in control, in a place that was a microcosm of Middle America, remote from the sophisticated metropolis.

"This is the West. When the legend becomes a fact, print the legend," declares a newspaper editor in *The Man Who Shot Liberty Valance*, John Ford's elegy to the frontier. Hollywood did just that, creating a reel illusion that seemed more real than everyday life, and a pantheon of stars who became more familiar than friends and neighbors.

"Make it big, do it right, give it class," was the motto at Metro-Goldwyn-Mayer, most opulent of the dream factories. Within its walls, and those of Paramount and Fox, Universal and Warners, Columbia and RKO, were contained many of the elements to be found in a city. In *Mayer and Thalberg: the Make-believe Saints*, Sam Marx, former head of the MGM Story Department, recalls the studio in its glory days, when 5000 worked there, and it boasted "more stars than there are in heaven":

"Early in the morning, actors and actresses appeared in the wardrobe department and the makeup building on Lot One, gulped coffee at the commissary counter; extras hastened to large sheds for their costumes and instructions. Outside the gate, itinerant workers clustered around in hopes that they would be needed as additional extras."

"On the stages, directors and cameramen surveyed their sets—some con-structed during the intermission of night—planned their camera setups and how to light them. Even when these chores were performed the previous night, after the day's shooting had ended, the director might have 'slept on it' and changed his plans."

"The studio population grew from nine o'clock on, with the arrival of the higher executive echelon and their staffs, members of the publicity department, writers, composers and all the creative forces that shaped the events of the future. There was a hospital and a barbershop."

"Technicians populated the paint, plaster and carpenter shops, the great prop building and a huge storing dock where unused backdrops were piled together, to be hauled out and repainted when needed again.

"A realistic waterfront was a permanent outdoor set. Overhead, an ingenious system of movable barrels could be turned upside down as fast as water was pumped into them, cascading mountainous waves onto the actors below. In this manner, raging storms were created under the California sun."

"Lot Two was entirely devoted to the outdoors; a skein of jungle rivers; massive rocks of the Stone Age; a French railway depot with European-type trains waiting on tracks that stretched away for all of a hundred yards; and streets of a small village stood back to back with those of New York."

Then there were three more lots; today, Metro-Goldwyn-Mayer occupies one office building across from the original Lot One now owned by Lorimar Telepictures, together with all of the facilities described above. But the commissary still serves the chicken soup made to the recipe of Louis B. Mayer's mother, which was introduced to encourage writers to stay on the lot and out of the neighborhood bars!

The experience of moviegoing soon matched the splendor of the studios. Sid Grauman and "Roxy" Rothafel commissioned architects to create dream palaces in which audiences could spend an evening of enchantment amid glittering decor, lights, music and—as the cherry on the cake—a movie on the screen. The show began on the sidewalk, beneath a vast marquee. Patrons were invited to wait in the lobby, amid chandeliers and white marble columns, gilded cherubs and carpets fit for royalty. There might be a string quartet, even complimentary refreshments, and a nurse to take care of the children.

Inside a vast auditorium (and even the smaller cities had palaces that were part of the studio chains), the customer was transported to another world: an evocation of Tut's Tomb, a Persian garden, the Paris Opera. The lights dimmed, stars twinkled overhead, the mighty Wurlitzer rose from its pit. At Grauman's Egyptian and Chinese Theaters, on Hollywood Boulevard, there were stage spectaculars keyed to the theme of the feature attraction, with dancers, singers and a full pit orchestra. Radio City Music Hall's Christmas Show is the last reminder of this extravagant era.

Critics dismissed such experiences as shallow escapism, an opium that distracted people from the real world. Today, those gaudy settings, like the weekly ritual of movie-going, seem as remote as Camelot, but the best pictures still bring out the audiences.

At every stage in their history, movies have functioned as a magic carpet, transporting us to the next town or, with equal ease, to galaxies far away and long ago. They have opened up new vistas, sharpened our appreciation of the familiar, brought us together as a people, mirrored our hopes and fears. Created collectively for a mass audience, they have reached for the universal and timeless and have also achieved the opposite: a priceless sense of a specific time and place, of shared values and conflicts.

Writers, producers and directors have shaped a medium whose visible manifestation is the image of the actor on screen. For much of this century, stars have filled the role of gods and goddesses for a secular society. A few of them have achieved mythic dimensions, surviving death to embody laughter, beauty or the spirit of an era.

Often it is the short-lived career that leaves the strongest mark. Rudolph Valentino and Clara Bow made but a handful of uneven pictures, yet they express our image of the twenties more vividly than actors who were more profound and durable—such as Lillian Gish and Buster Keaton. Jean Harlow, Humphrey Bogart and Marilyn Monroe each stands for a decade, just as Garbo symbolizes unattainable beauty, and Cary Grant suave humor, even to the youngest of moviegoers.

This is but one example of Hollywood's cunning in subverting our defenses and appealing to our fantasies. Even today, movies serve as shorthand. We refer casually to the Strategic Defense Initiative as *Star Wars,* to the baby boomers as *The Big Chill* generation, to Bernard Goetz as a *Death Wish* vigilante, to a *Rambo* foreign policy. Phrases become a part of common speech, sometimes for years: "Take him for a ride," "Make him a proposition he can't refuse," "I'm mad as hell and I'm not going to take it any more," among them. People still talk of a *Walter Mitty* personality, forty years after the movie popularized the James Thurber story.

From the twenties on, Hollywood has been an arbiter of taste. Everyone knows the story that, when Clark Gable revealed a bare torso in *It Happened One Night,* the sales of men's undershirts dropped precipitously. A decade earlier, Douglas Fairbanks had made the suntanned, mustachioed athlete a beau ideal, as Colleen Moore had encouraged young women to tape up their breasts, shingle their hair and roll their stockings. The influence of stars peaked in the thirties, when times were hard and distractions few; when pleasures had to be enjoyed vicariously. Marlene Dietrich started a run on slacks, Carole Lombard popularized lounging pajamas, Dorothy Lamour speeded acceptance of the sarong. Wire-haired terriers were given a boost by *The Thin Man;* little girls were dressed to look like Shirley Temple.

Ironically, vintage Hollywood now shapes the work of European couturiers, who see the classics—often for the first time—revived on television. The top Italian menswear designers are inspired by the dapper suits worn by Gary Cooper and Fred Astaire, and try to capture the look of those "happy and successful heroes," as Nino Cerruti put it. Yves St. Laurent sees *Gilda,* and Rita Hayworth's strapless back satin dance dress is reborn as Paris couture. Even in recent years, Hollywood has launched fashions and fads, with movies as varied as *Bonnie and Clyde* and *Flashdance, Urban Cowboy* and *Annie Hall.*

Entire genres of films have mirrored and helped shape the national consensus—none more so than the Western. From the first fragments of Wild West shows, shot in Fort Lee, New Jersey, through epics of the frontier and singing cowboys in white hats, to revisionist accounts of the Indian wars, to adventures in the Bronx and outer space: the Western has evolved as a vehicle of American mythology, and has had an impact around the world. German-born Henry Kissinger admitted to Italian journalist Oriana Fallaci: "I've always acted alone. Americans admire the cowboy leading the caravan alone, the cowboy entering a village alone on his horse...a Wild West tale, if you like."

Austrian-born psychologist Bruno Bettelheim expressed a different view:

"The Westerns gave us the feeling of wide open spaces, of the unlimited opportunities this wilderness offered to man, and the inherent challenge to bring civilization to places where there had been none. The same movies also suggested the danger of chaos; the wagon train symbolized the community of man, the community man must form for such a perilous journey into the untamed wilderness—which also referred to all that is untamed within ourselves. The Western gave us a vision of the need for cooperation and civilization, because without it, man would perish."

The loner and the community, *The Searchers* and *Wagonmaster:* Hollywood played variations on these themes long after the frontier was closed and the experience of taming it receded into history. But in *Star Wars,* there is again an open frontier, and Bettelheim suggests that:

"Science fiction movies can serve as myths about the future, and thereby give us some assurance about it...Such movies tell about tremendous progress which will expand man's powers and his experience beyond anything now believed possible. But they assure us, on the other hand, that all these advances will not obliterate man or life as we now know it, (that) man's basic concerns will be the same, and the struggle of good against evil, the central moral problem of all times, will not have lost its importance."

The influence of the movies has always been challenged. In their earliest years, the *Chicago Tribune* thundered that they were without redeeming features and that it would be proper to ban them at once. In the early twenties, Fatty Arbuckle was made the scapegoat for the real and imagined sins of Hollywood, and Will Hays, then the Postmaster General, was called in to clean it up. In the thirties, the Payne Report offered pseudo-scientific proof that the movies were turning our children into hardened criminals and moral degenerates. Rock'n'roll in the fifties, pornography in the seventies, and ultra-violence today have also come under attack.

Foreigners are considered especially susceptible to corruption. Declared *Time* in 1950:

> *"Probably the deepest trouble of the contemporary U.S. is its inability to produce a reasonably accurate image of itself. In plays, movies, novels, it cruelly caricatures its life, parades its vices, mutes its excellences. This tendency, far more than Communist propaganda, is responsible for the repulsive picture of U.S. life in the minds of many Europeans and Asians."*

Producer Walter Wanger had a more detached view. He saw Hollywood as America's finest ambassador, producing movies that offered: "a perpetual epic of the ordinary, unregimented individual—who chooses a profession, travels at will, outguesses the boss and wisecracks the government."

The balance of evidence suggests that American movies have won more friends abroad than have our politicians, and that their influence may be more favorable than we have any right to expect. Joseph Goebbels, Hitler's Minister of Propaganda, would have loved to have had Frank Capra working for him, and audiences in occupied Europe ignored the irreverence that enraged official Washington, and cheered Mr. Smith. Akira Kurosawa in Japan saw *The Grapes of Wrath,* and later declared that he knew then that no nation capable of producing such a picture could be defeated. In China, three decades of virulent anti-American propaganda failed to obliterate memories of Hollywood movies; SRO crowds thronged classic revivals, which were presented day and night until the prints wore out. "How is Clark Gable?," American visitors were asked.

In Mussolini's Italy, attendance at American pictures was discouraged, and so Vittorio de Sica played surrogate, modelling himself on such Hollywood stars as Leslie Howard and William Powell. In a remote Brazilian mining town, the dummies in a store window are of Laurel and Hardy. Parisians are still infatuated with Chaplin, and Woody Allen is a hot ticket. Japanese architect Arata Isozaki designed a "Marilyn Monroe" chair, its high laddered back describing a sinuous curve, and used that same curve to enliven the geometric structure of his Museum of Contemporary Art in Los Angeles.

Professionals share the delight of moviegoers. Jeanne Moreau cast Keith Carradine in her first directorial feature, *Lumière,* to play a rangy, laconic American "like Gary Cooper." Director Sergio Leone, who launched the career of Clint Eastwood in Italian-made Westerns, declared: "I love the vast spaces of John Ford and the metropolitan claustrophobia of Martin Scorsese, the alternating petals of the American daisy."

Perhaps the highest tribute that can be paid to Hollywood, is that so many established foreign directors and stars, cameramen and designers want to work here. In doing so, they continue a tradition that began with Charlie Chaplin and Charles Rosher (both from London), Mary Pickford (from Toronto) and Ben Carré (from Paris). And they continue to enrich American filmmaking. Nestor Almendros (from Cuba) wins plaudits for his cinematography in *Kramer vs Kramer* and *Sophie's Choice,* as does Miroslav Ondricek (from Czechoslovakia) for his collaborations with compatriot Milos Forman on *Ragtime* and *Amadeus.* Many of these emigrés become so much a part of the mainstream that, like the other 240 million emigré stock who people these United States, they cease to attract attention. The important thing is that the talent keeps coming.

It is also a sign that some things never change. The movies have come a long way since Griffith and De Mille made their first pictures in Hollywood, and the town has altered beyond recognition. Back then, motion pictures were disreputable, but cheap to make and sure to please. Now they are studied by 30,000 students a year; produced and distributed by MBAs. But they are fearsomely expensive to make, and even the most experienced executive is often not certain which ones—if any—will make money. Moviemaking has become a high-stakes lottery.

In the studio era, talent was moved around like chess pieces; each piece had its defined moves, and the moguls did the moving. In general, writers wrote what their bosses assigned; actors accepted their roles or went on suspension; directors were handed a script the day before shooting began. Now, every player, high and low, has the freedom to do what he wants. One picture, unless it's a smash, is no guarantee that another will follow.

The essentials have shifted very little. The last major change in the technique of making movies was the coming of sound, sixty years ago. The filmmakers who mastered that revolution would have no problem in adjusting to the equipment now in use. The very first movies were made by tiny crews. The same person might write the story, assign the parts, direct the actors and edit the picture. Warren Beatty and Woody Allen still do—with a little help from their friends. The only difference is that these all-rounders take their time on every feature, whereas the pioneers cheerfully cranked out unpretentious shorts at the rate of one or more a week.

Story-telling probably began with the caveman, and moviemaking occupies a fragment of time at the end of this long history. So it is not surprising that the basic plots and genres have been constantly recycled, and that the basic ingredients of a fast-paced, gripping narrative, with lively characterizations, enlivened by humor or pathos, thrills or romance—or all of the above—are as valid today as they were at the start. Buster Keaton dodging boulders and a racing train to reach the church in time; Bullitt pursuing his quarry in a souped-up Mustang over the hills of San Francisco; E.T. eluding his pursuers on an airborne bike: the nail-biting suspense, and sense of catharsis as the hero comes through, are identical from one decade to the next.

What has changed is the way we look at movies. Watching oversized images in a darkened theater amid strangers who shared collective emotions, was a more potent experience than catching them in fragments on television, or plugging in a cassette. Something was lost when theater-going declined. Then, movies were a familiar treat, but a little removed from everyday life; now they are easily accessible and lacking in mystery.

The one unquestioned benefit of cassettes is that everyone can enjoy what was once the privilege of a few archivists: a library of motion picture landmarks. Looking back may encourage us to look forward, to realize how precious the medium is, and how great a contribution it can still make to our lives.

Happy Birthday, Hollywood! It was always the name that mattered, even when the action moved to Burbank and Culver City. And now that it has moved further—to Astoria in Queens, to Marin County and Wilmington, N.C.—Hollywood still has the ring of magic, here and everywhere. "This is the West. When the legend becomes a fact, print the legend."

Hollywood stands for personal vision, craftsmanship and the passion to communicate with a large audience, as well as the bottom line. Let a master of those skills have the last word. Billy Wilder offers a message of hope to his fellow artists:

> *"I've been here for fifty years, and all through those years I've watched Tinsel Town vacillate between despair and fear. First it's going to be sound that will kill us, then it was television, then cable, then pornography, then cassettes; and now that terrifying new word— microchips...microchips that will supplant the human brain—and the human heart. Mechanical gadgets that can simulate emotions, dreams, laughter, tears. Well, so far they have not succeeded. Not yet, anyway. So, relax, fellow picturemakers. We are not expendable. The bigger they get, the more irreplaceable we become. Theirs may be the kingdom, but ours is the power and the glory."*

1

The First Decade
1887-1897

In the beginning, Hollywood is one of a hundred struggling communities that are created on paper during the great land boom of 1886-87. California has been a magic name since the Gold Rush of 1849; an El Dorado to lure pioneers across the continent.

Editor Horace Greeley did not say, "Go West, young man, go West," but plenty of others did, and the call was heeded. By the 1870s, Los Angeles urgently needs settlers; drought has put an end to ranching; its population has dropped in five years from 16,000 to 11,000. Just as the rust belt solicits high tech industry today, so does Los Angeles seek to attract farmers. Boosters range the nation, extolling an earthly paradise, "where every man may sit under his own vine and fig tree."

What is needed is cheap and easy access. The Southern Pacific Railroad arrives in 1881, but the one-way fare from the Mississippi Valley is $100, a tariff only the affluent can afford. In 1885, a competing line, the Atchison, Topeka and Santa Fe, makes a connection, and a price war erupts. For one day in the spring of 1886, the Southern Pacific offers a ticket from Kansas City for a dollar.

Even at $25, the trip is a bargain, and the immigrants flood in on every train. Hotels are jammed; guests sleep head to head on cots, in bathtubs or in tents. Everybody is selling land to everybody else. Visitors are met at the depot by brass bands, and banners depict lush orchards and fertile fields. Orators and handbills seek to persuade that "the first duty of man is to buy a lot."

Newspapers are full of advertisements, of which this is a fair sample:

TUSTIN
The Beautiful
Unexcelled in Charm and Loveliness
An Earthly Eden Unsurpassed in
Wealth of Flower and Foliage
However, Imagination Cannot Conceive It
It must be Seen to be Realized!

Most of the new arrivals are not farmers, but middle-aged city dwellers looking for a new home, a warm climate for their declining years, or the opportunity to gamble on rising land prices. Prices shoot up, five-fold in a year, and more land is brought onto the market, subdivided and auctioned off. At first, there are excursion buses, and the offer of "a free ride and a free lunch" lures hobos and spectators who have come to have a good time.

Later, it becomes a sellers' market, as frenzied buyers stand in line to put down a payment on property they have never seen in order to resell it for a profit, or to sell their place in line to a late arrival. Ditch diggers and cleaning women scrape together enough to enter the race.

In three months in the summer of 1887, $100 million changes hands in recorded sales—and many are not recorded. Prospectuses do not mention where these "choice building sites" are located. Desert land is bought for $20 an acre and sold for $800. Lots are laid out on inaccessible mountain tops and advertised for their dramatic views. Undrained swamps are sold on the basis of their abundant water supply. Locals learn the fine arts of hyperbole and exaggeration, long before movie publicists refine the techniques.

By April 1888, the banks begin to restrain credit, and the boom collapses. But the boosters' original goal has been achieved. Substantial improvements are made in downtown Los Angeles. The population decline is reversed and every decade for the next 100 years brings a spectacular growth of population.

Two thirds of the new towns laid out during the boom vanish from the map, often before their first properties are built. Morocco, the forerunner of Beverly Hills, and Sherman, which occupied the present site of West Hollywood, are among the casualties.

Hollywood—then, as throughout its history—is a survivor. It comprises a 120 acre tract in the Cahuenga valley, a fraction of what goes by the name today. The founders name it after an estate near Chicago and intend that it should be a sober, God-fearing community, with churches, school and a library, but no saloons or theaters. With the poetic license so characteristic of Los Angeles realtors, the first map of the tract carries a handsome rendering of the Hotel Hollywood—16 years before that hostelry is built.

Far removed from this sleepy outpost, inventors conduct the experiments that lead to the birth of motion pictures. Movies are the culmination of a century of experiments: of panoramas and magic lanterns, of oddly-named devices such as the zoetrope, praxinoscope and phenakistiscope.

Thomas Edison is given much of the credit. "When I invented the modern moving picture in the summer of 1889," he later announced to the press, "I sought to do for the eye what the phonograph had done for the ear. The high character of the pictures made by my own companies and the other American and foreign companies under my own patents represent a development that has far exceeded my most ambitious hope." It is an impressive claim.

The goal, in the United States and Europe, is to create a mechanism that will achieve the illusion of movement in combination with photography. Within a few years, the goal is attained. Edison is first with a viewer; the Lumière brothers premiere movie projection.

The Lumières' father, Antoine, is skeptical. A Parisian magician, Georges Meliès, is bowled over by the first demonstration and offers a fortune in gold to buy the invention. Antoine refuses. "Young man, you'll thank me," he tells Meliès. "My sons' invention is not for sale. It would ruin you. It can be exploited for a short while as a scientific curiosity. Beyond that, it has no commercial future." Within a month, the audience proves him wrong, and the Lumières earn $10 million dollars in just five years from this uncommercial invention.

1887 Hollywood appears on the map, as Harvey Wilcox, a successful realtor and ardent prohibitionist from Kansas, registers his subdivision on February 1st. His wife, Daeida, hears a woman on the train describe an estate called Hollywood, and she suggests that this would be a good name for the new venture. All attempts to cultivate English holly fail; however, Harvey is more conscientious than most developers of the day. When the boom fails and sales lag, he gives up his fine house in downtown Los Angeles and moves to a modest ranch house in Hollywood. He plants pepper trees along the streets and, during a drought when water is scarce, breaks watermelons on their roots to keep them alive. The first settlers in Hollywood plant a lemon grove.

In Philadelphia, Eadweard Muybridge, an English-born inventor, publishes "Animal Locomotion," serial photographs of movement that anticipates motion pictures. His work has been stimulated by a commission from California Governor Leland Stanford, industrialist and founder of Stanford University. Stanford is eager to win a bet that a galloping horse may lift all four legs from the ground at once.

Muybridge arranges 24 still cameras in a row along a track and attaches each camera's shutter to an electronic trip wire distributor developed by Southern Pacific Railroad mechanical engineer John D. Isaacs. A galloping horse trips each wire in turn and is thus recorded in a sequence of movements. Muybridge continues his experiments, with animals and humans, improving his techniques to the point where they influence such motion picture pioneers as Edison and, in France, Etienne-Jules Marey.

1889 Edison's assistant, W.K.L. Dickson, begins work on the Kinetophone, a device that is intended to show short films in conjunction with a phonograph recording.

1891 Edison patents the Kinetoscope, a peep-show device through which one can view a sequence of moving images.

Harvey Wilcox dies. His widow, Daeida manages his real estate interests, energetically fostering the growth of Hollywood, until her death in 1919. She donates land for churches, city hall and a library, and establishes the first bank.

1892 Successful demonstration of the Kinetograph camera and Kinetoscope viewer. Both use George Eastman's newly-invented celluloid film, whose 35mm stock is perforated to the same standard as today's. The Kinetoscope is marketed as a penny-in-the-slot attraction, and Kinetoscope parlors spring up in major cities. However, the Kinetograph weighs over 1100 pounds, and requires an electrical power source, limiting its mobility.

1893 Dickson constructs the "Black Maria," the world's first movie studio, near Edison's laboratories at Orange, N.J. It is a large box, covered with black tar paper. Part of the roof can be removed to admit sunlight and the whole structure is mounted on a turntable to follow the sun throughout the day. Its name is popular slang for a paddy wagon, which it resembles.

Vaudeville and circus artists are invited to perform a part of their routines on the tiny stage. Annie Oakley and Colonel Cody are among the first performers. The first recorded picture, *Fred Ott's Sneeze*, features a studio employee with a luxuriant mustache delivering one of his trademark sneezes, a feat that is stimulated during the shooting with pepper and snuff.

1894 One of the big productions at the Black Maria is *Bucking Bronco,* which runs about 30 seconds and employs members of Buffalo Bill's Wild West Show, which was then on tour in Orange, N.J. Another is *Fun in a Chinese Laundry,* which gives its name, 60 years later, to the autobiography of director Josef von Sternberg.

1895 French inventors Louis & Auguste Lumière patent the *Cinématographe,* a combined camera/contact printer/projector, which weighs only 10 pounds. It is hand-cranked and, in contrast to Edison's behemoth, can be used to shoot in the streets; then to process the film; and, in conjunction with an arc lantern, to project the result.

The Lumières present the first commercial screening on December 28 at a café on the Boulevard des Capucines in Paris. (They have been turned down by the Musee Grévin, a waxworks, and by the Folies Bérgères.) The program includes minute-long sequences of workers leaving the Lumière factory in Lyon, Auguste Lumière feeding his baby daughter, and a little improvised comedy in which a naughty boy tricks a gardener into dousing himself with a hose and is punished for the prank. The big sensation is a sequence showing a train pulling into La Ciotat station. Early audiences gasp, fearing that the train will burst through the screen.

1896 Edison holds his first public screening on April 23 at Koster and Bial's Music Hall, a New York vaudeville house. His counterpart of the Lumières' train is a shot of breaking waves, which has a dramatic effect in frightening nervous spectators.

In the same year, Edison produces the first recorded piece of motion picture erotica titled, *The Widow Jones.* It includes a 20-second kiss by a homely couple, John C. Rice and May Irwin.

In his social history, "The Lively Audience," Russell Lynes describes the howls of indignation this modest picture provoked. "The clergy denounced it as, 'a lyric of the stockyards'. *Chap Book,* a small Chicago magazine, said: 'The spectacle of the prolonged pasturing on each other's lips was hard to bear. When only life size, it was pronounced beastly (it was a scene from a play). Magnified to Gargantuan proportions and repeated three times over it is absolutely disgusting...such things call for police interference.'"

For the next few years, movies are shown as a novelty attraction in vaudeville houses to generate larger audiences for live entertainment, or by travelling fairground showmen in "Electric Theaters" and "Bioscopes."

The Lumières, the world's largest manufacturer of photographic products after George Eastman in Rochester, put their invention to practical use, sending cameramen around the world in search of fresh material. These first documentary subjects include the coronation of Czar Nicholas II, the Brooklyn Bridge, and the canals of Venice—filmed from a moving gondola.

Colonel Griffith (born Griffith J. Griffith in Glamorgan, South Wales) donates 3000 acres of land in Los Feliz, north-east of Hollywood, to create a park in his name. When the first moviemakers arrive, it proves a popular location, and D.W. Griffith (who is unrelated to the Colonel) shoots his Civil war battle scenes for *The Birth of a Nation* in wilder parts of the park. Later still, Julius Stern, a producer of low-budget comedies, refuses to allow an ambitious director to go further afield: "A rock is a rock, a tree is a tree; shoot it in Griffith Park," he declares.

1887 Harvey Wilcox, a successful midwestern land developer, purchases land at the foot of Cahuenga pass.

A tribute from
American Broadcasting
Company

*1887   Daeida Wilcox
names her husband's real
estate adventure,
Hollywood.*

ca. 1887 The Blondeau Tavern, at the northwest corner of Sunset Boulevard and Gower Street became Hollywood's first movie studio in 1911.

A tribute from
John Gary Coakley,
President, J.C. Backings
Corporation

*1888   Harvey Wilcox's first
advertisement for the
Hollywood properties.*

ca. 1890   An early kineti-
scope machine using
photographs on a cylinder.
It was later developed for
use with film.

*ca. 1893   Edison's 'Black
Maria,' considered the first
motion picture studio in the
United States.*

ca. 1895 Thomas Armat, motion picture inventor, develops the "beater" projector which establishes the essential timing between each frame of film. All screen projection depends upon this intermittent film movement.

1895   Louis and Auguste Lumiere, who presented the first public screening of motion pictures in Paris, using the Cinematographe, a combined camera, printer and projector. Photographed at Lyon, France.

THE WONDERFUL MUTOSCOPE SHOWING

MOVING PICTURES PHOTOGRAPHED FROM LIFE

ca. 1895 An early advertisement for one of Edison's Mutoscope productions.

SANDOW

The Famous Strong Man and Athletic Marvel of the Country, in his Great Muscular Exhibition.

A tribute from
Allan Levine and The Hand
Prop Room, Inc.

1896   Edison produces the
first recorded piece of
motion picture "erotica,"
"The Widow Jones" (aka
"The Kiss"). It provoked the
first calls for censorship.

ca. 1897 Due to Edison's reluctance to continue developing motion picture technology, W. L. K. Dickson left the Edison employ to found a rival company, the American Mutoscope & Biographic Co. Shown here with camera crew preparing to shoot the Jeffries-Sharkey fight, Coney Island, New York, in 1899.

A tribute from
Andy McIntyre and the
AME family of companies

ca. 1897   The Biograph Studio, 841 Broadway, New York, builds the first rooftop motion picture studio. It was designed to revolve with the sun.

ca. 1897   Thomas L. Tally brings the first motion picture to Los Angeles at his Phonograph Parlor on South Spring Street. It was called a "peep-show" because people were afraid to go into a darkened theater. They stood outside peeping at the screen through eye holes.

*ca. 1897 Hollywood
began as a rural com-
munity of conservative
farmers.*

ca. 1897 One of Hollywood's first farms near Franklin Avenue and Beechwood Drive.

A tribute from
Hollywood Health Care
Clinic

ca. 1872 California Governor Leland Stanford hires photographer Eadweard Muybridge to devise a means of photographing a horse in motion. Stanford had made a large bet involving the gait of one of his race horses but it was not until 1878 that Stanford and Muybridge finally incorporated the engineering expertise of John D. Issacs and his electronic shutter tripping system to actually make the photograph.

1878   The section of the racetrack where John D. Issac's electronic shutter tripping system was connected to Muybridge's 24-camera installation to photograph Leland Stanford's race horse, "Sallie Gardner."

A tribute from
Consolidated Film
Industries (CFI)

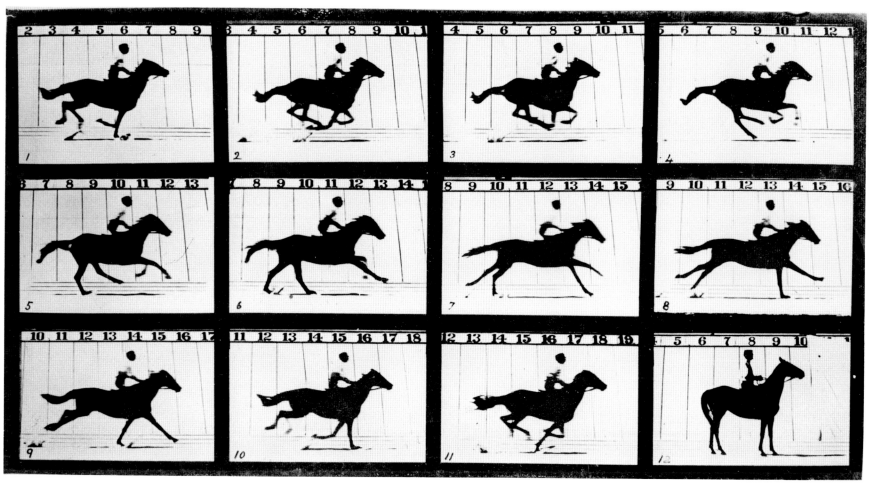

*1878   California Governor,
Leland Stanford, wins his
wager made years before,
that all four hooves of his
race horse leave the ground
while running.*

2

The Second Decade 1897-1907

Hollywood grows in leisurely fashion. A few ornate mansions are built along Prospect Avenue, which is later renamed Hollywood Boulevard. Horses and carriages are still the principal form of transportation. Streets are dusty and unpaved, but tranquil and shady.

The first post office is established in 1897 in Mr. Sackett's Hotel and Emporium at the corner of Prospect and Cahuenga Avenue. It is a great convenience for residents, who had formerly to collect their mail from the main office, seven miles away. The Women's Club raises funds for the purchase of books and the building of Hollywood's first public library. An electric trolley crosses sheep pastures, bean fields and citrus orchards on its way to downtown Los Angeles.

Goodwin and Bynon, Hollywood's first real estate office, is established in 1899. Land fever has begun to rise again. A salesman shows a client a two-acre plot fronting on Prospect Avenue. The price is $400, and the client decides that that is too high. A month later, the salesman tries again; the price is now $600. Again the client refuses. Another month passes, and this time the client makes the call. The price has risen again, to $800. Declares the impatient customer: "My! That's a bitter pill to swallow, but I believe I'll take it," and hands over his deposit.

Two years later, there is another boom, as the Ocean View tract to the north and east of Hollywood, is put on the market. Its backers intend that this should be an exclusive neighborhood. They stipulate that there shall be no multiple dwellings and no house costing less than $3500 on any plot. Roads are laid out with curbs and ornamental trees.

The Hollywood Hotel, long anticipated, is finally built, in Mission-revival style. To celebrate its opening, a barbecue is held and every important citizen is invited to make a speech. The oratory ends with a pithy observation from General Moses H. Sherman, who gestures grandly towards the burgeoning town and declares: "Behold what God hath wrought!"

Los Angeles enjoys an oil boom, doubling its population to 250,000, in the years 1900 to 1907. Its outlying communities are linked by the Red Car. Venice and Santa Monica are thriving seaside resorts; Ocean Park is the West Coast's answer to Coney Island.

In "Southern California: an Island on the Land," historian Carey McWilliams describes Los Angeles as "the most priggish community in America after 1900," in contrast to its reputation before 1870 as "the toughest town in the nation." He quotes a contemporary observer, Willard Huntington Wright, who explains in a magazine, *The Smart Set*, that the city's character has been formed by the "rural pietist obsessed with the spirit of village fellowship, of suburban respectability...During the early morning hours no frou-frou of silk disturbs the sepulchral silence of the streets. You will look in vain for the flashing eye, the painted cheek, the silken ankle...The current belief in Los Angeles is that there is something inherently and inalienably indecent (or at least indelicate) in that segment of the day between 12 midnight and 5 am...Hence, the recent illumination and guarding of all public parks lest spooning, that lewd pastime, become prevalent. Hence, the Quakerish regulation of the public dance halls. Hence, a stupid censorship so incredibly puerile that even Boston will have to take second place. Hence, the silly legal pottering about the proper length of bathing suits at the beaches, the special election to decide whether or not one should be permitted to eat in saloons, and the fiery discussion as to the morality of displaying moving pictures of boxing matches. Los Angeles is overrun with militant moralists, connoisseurs of sin, experts of biological purity."

After saloons, the greatest affront to these moralists is motion picture exhibition. The movies establish a firm hold on the affections of the urban working class, and particularly the vast immigrant populations of New York, Chicago and Philadelphia, which become the major centers of production, distribution and exhibition. It is the immigrants who respond to the hunger of their fellow outsiders for cheap, accessible entertainment. They are a part of the mass audience, and their taste and entreprenurial skills transform the "flickers" into a flourishing business.

The first purpose-built movie theaters, christened nickelodeons (for the price of admission), are built in the working-class neighborhoods of major cities. They draw crowds, all day every day, and proliferate: by the end of the decade, it is estimated that there are over 10,000 small and unsanitary theaters. Early shows run 15 minutes, plus song slides. Later, hour-long programs of shorts with live piano accompaniment are presented for a dime. The Warner brothers, William Fox, Louis B. Mayer and Adolph Zukor begin their motion picture careers as theater owners; Jack Warner's specialty is singing—so badly as to empty the house for the next performance.

1897 The Lubin Company of Philadelphia recreates the Corbett-Fitzsimmons prizefight, using two freight handlers from the Pennsylvania Railroad. The Vitagraph Company produces *The Burglar on the Roof*, which runs under a minute and budgeted at $3.50, in its rooftop studio in Lower Manhattan. Another major release is *Fatima*, a close-up of the famed Coney Island belly dancer.

American producers seek protection against the inroads of European moviemakers, who are better organized and artistically more advanced. Lumière cameramen are arrested for filming without a permit in New York's Central Park, and are released only through the intervention of the French Ambassador.

1898 Patriotic fervor runs high as Spain declares war on the United States, in an attempt to hold its colonies in Cuba and the Philippines. J. Stuart Blackton makes an inflammatory picture, *Tearing Down the Spanish Flag*. But the propaganda triumph of the year is made by E.H. Amet for Vitagraph. Titled: *The Sinking of Admiral Cervera's Fleet by the U.S. Atlantic Squadron in Santiago Harbor*, it purports to show the celebrated night battle, filmed live with a unique, super-sensitive "moonlight" film. In fact, Amet has built a scale model of Santiago Harbor; made cut-outs of the battleships, and has filmed them in a bathtub, using cigarette smoke to suggest explosions.

1899 Rivalry between the many competing film companies in New York becomes intense. The Biograph Company sets up powerful lights in order to film the Jeffries-Sharkey heavyweight bout on Coney Island. Its cameramen occupy the front row. Twenty rows back, a crew from Vitagraph are pirating the fight. They are spotted, Pinkerton men are dispatched to seize the cameras, but the spectators take sides and foil the pursuers. The Vitagraph crew return to their studios to process their film. That night it is stolen by representatives of the Edison Company.

1900 First Hollywood sightseeing bus begins operation.

1901 Hollywood's first artist, French-born Paul de Longpré, settles on Cahuenga Avenue, purchasing three lots on which to build a luxurious house and garden. For his studio, he acquires a corner lot from Daeida Wilcox, in exchange for three canvases. The De Longpré house and garden soon become the top local tourist attraction, for his floral paintings are widely admired, and his hospitality is renowned.

1902 An amusement arcade in downtown Los Angeles becomes the first American cinema, when owner Thomas Tally removes the peep shows, installs seats and a projector, and names it the "Electric Theatre." Four years later he built the New Broadway Theater, C.A.'s first custom-designed movie house. It is this theater that can be glimpsed in Harold Lloyd's *Safety Last*, which uses a "high rise" building at the corner of Sixth Street and Broadway for its celebrated cliff-hanging finale.

Georges Meliès, a magician turned trick filmmaker, plans a documentary of the Coronation of King Edward VII in London. Denied admission to the ceremony, he stages it in Paris. Later, the King sees the film and reportedly expresses appreciation for Meliès' skill in recreating those parts of the ritual that were eliminated from the actual service.

Meliès deserves much of the credit for the development of theatrical pictures. A flamboyant stage magician, who utilized a magic lantern as part of his visual sorcery, he is first in line to buy the Lumières' *Cinématographe*. When they turn him down, he purchases a Bioscope projector from English inventor Robert Paul, constructs his own camera, and begins filming novelty items in the streets, much as the Lumière cameramen are doing. One day, as he is shooting in Paris, the camera jams, and a few seconds elapse before he can restart it. The scene has changed and so, when the film is processed, he sees that a carriage has apparently been transformed into a hearse.

Inspired by this accident, he builds the first European film studio, at Montreuil (a replica of which has been constructed in the German Film Museum in Frankfurt). It allows him to refine his techniques and to create a series of trick films that offer a more elaborate version of his stage shows. They include *The One Man Band*, in which Meliès himself appears as seven different characters in the same frame of film; *Joan of Arc*, which employs 500 extras; *A Trip to the Moon*, his most celebrated production, which is still revived; and *The Conquest of the Pole*, one of his last and most ambitious, made in 1912, before bankruptcy puts an end to his career as a filmmaker.

Meliès' pictures are widely distributed and inspire imitators. An Edwin S. Porter production, *The Happy Hooligan and the Airship*, shows a man riding a bicycle, suspended beneath a balloon that floats over New York.

1903 Hollywood, with a population of about 1000, votes for incorporation as a city of the sixth class. The contest is a close one: 88 in favor and 77 opposed. A stream of regulations is promulgated. The sale of liquor is forbidden, except on prescription from a pharmacist. Games of chance and slot machines are likewise barred. It is forbidden to shoot rabbits from the rear platform of a streetcar, or to drive more than 2000 sheep, goats or hogs down any street, unless a specified number of competent men are in charge. A final prohibition is directed against the riding of bicycles on Hollywood's two sidewalks.

Two mansions survive from this first era of civic growth. The Janes House is the last private house on Hollywood Boulevard between Vermont and La Brea Avenues. For 15 years it is an elementary school, run by the three daughters of the first owner, Herman Janes. Its roster includes the children of Cecil B. De Mille, Jesse Lasky, Thomas Ince, Noah Beery and Richard Arlen. Later it falls on hard times and is nearly lost, but it is now (in 1987) to become a tourist information office.

A block north of the Chinese Theater, on the corner of Franklin and Orange, is a Spanish-style stucco house, which houses the American Society of Cinematographers. Visitors can explore the fine collection of cameras and other memorabilia that the Society maintains. The Hollywood Hotel, long an institution and host to Louella Parsons' celebrated broadcasts, was demolished in 1956. Also gone are Glengarry Castle, with its marble statues, authentic armor, tapestries and antique furniture; and Sans Souci, which was modeled on Rhineland castles and the baronial halls of medieval England. Both were built by a retired Chicago doctor, A.G. Schloesser, who changed his name to Castle at the outbreak of war to escape anti-German prejudice.

Edwin S. Porter makes one of the first action adventures, *The Life of an American Fireman.* Fire is a recurrent threat in crowded theaters screening highly flammable nitrate film that unspools into an open basket, and Porter's tribute to the fireman's skill is both a natural dramatic subject and a welcome reassurance to nervous patrons.

Later in the year he produces an epic: a 12-minute Western drama, *The Great Train Robbery,* also in Edison's studio in lower Manhattan. Original prints are hand-colored and include a dramatic close-up of an outlaw taking aim and firing at the camera. Projectionists are advised that this close-up may be used to open or to end the picture. The first audience is so excited that it insists on the film being rerun several times.

Harry J. Miles, a cameraman, opens the first film exchange in New York, buying prints from producers and renting them to exhibitors. Until now, films have been sold outright to theater owners at so many cents a foot. So avid are audiences for novelty, that programs are changed at least twice a week, and a market develops in used pictures. Within four years, there are 100 such exchanges, a key step towards the distribution networks that will soon control and regulate production and exhibition.

1904 The year's clouded Crystal Ball Award goes to City Attorney Young, for a speech in which he declares: "Hollywood can never be a large business center, but it is being more and more recognized as a city of homes." The following year, the price of the city's best-situated land rises to $4000 an acre.

At the St. Louis Worlds Fair, a major draw is Hale's Tours and Scenes of the World. Visitors sit in a simulated railway carriage and watch film sequences of celebrated landmarks and landscapes through the windows.

1905 What is reputed to be the first nickelodeon is built in Pittsburgh.

1906 The first animated cartoon, *Humorous Phases of Funny Faces,* is created by the English-born pioneer J. Stuart Blackton in the world's first glass-enclosed studios, in Flatbush, Brooklyn. Versatile and innovative, Blackton is credited with many of the advances made during this formative era. Like Griffith, he emphasizes film editing—notably in *Scenes of True Life,* which he makes from 1908 on. He also creates a successful series of animated cartoons.

ca. 1897   The Edison Kinetoscope had been installed in what was known as "peep show" parlors before the advent of motion picture projection. Notice the transition from cylinder to film loop.

A tribute from
MTM

*ca. 1897   A Kinetoscope
Parlor in San Francisco
featuring Edison
novelty shorts.*

Farragut Theatre
TO-NIGHT
EDISON'S PROJECTOSCOPE
The 19th Century Marvel.

——AMONG THE VIEWS TO BE SHOWN——

Village Blacksmith
Portion of the Procession attending the Ceremonies at the Coronation of the Czar of Russia at Moscow
Loading a Coke Oven at Carmaux, France
March of the French African Soldiers
Juggler Trewry in his famous Ribbon Act
Arrival of Family
Aquarium
German Dragoons.
Hurdle Jumping.

Spanish Artillery
Chicago Police Parade
Tearing down an old Building
Street Dances, London
Whirlpool Rapids
Arrival of Fast Mail, Paris
Spanish Infantry
Game of Cards
Children at Play.
Gardner and Bad Boy
Quarreling Babies
Caravan of Camels, Egypt
Street in Cario
St. Marc, Venice
Russian Dance, Etc

Edison's wonderful Projectoscope will be seen at the Farragut Theatre one night only, Wednesday December 8th. This machine is without a doubt the best and most perfect ever shown to the public. Next to life itself nothing is so real as the Projectoscope. It reproduces nature and natural movements with such resemblance that confound the spectators who are obliged to believe that it is life itself that is before their eyes.

Special Low Prices; 15 cts, 25 cts and 35 cts
SEATS NOW ON SALE AT HARRIER & SON'S.
VALLEJO CHRONICLE PRINT.

1897 An independent exhibitor's handbill.

*ca. 1898   J. S. Blackton
and Albert Smith, of the
newly formed Vitagraph
Company, set up on the
steps of New York City Hall
to photograph Dewey's
return from Manila.*

ca. 1901 A scene from
Edison's "What Happened
on 23rd Street, New York"
was called a real "shocker"
for actually showing a
lady's knee.

A tribute from
Mr. and Mrs.
Sherwood Schwartz

ca. 1903   A precurser to
the cineplex theater
concept. Film was often
incorporated into sideshow
and circus acts.

PLEASE READ THE
Titles to yourself.
LOUD READING
ANNOYS YOUR
NEIGHBORS

Change
of Song
to-morrow

Just a moment
PLEASE
While The
OPERATOR
CHANGES A REEL.

ca. 1903   Early title cards
remind customers of
theater etiquette.

34

*1903 A scene from
Edison's "The Great Train
Robbery." Known as one of
the first "action adventure"
pictures in the United
States. It was 12 minutes
long, with a beginning, a
middle, and an end. The
first American epic.*

1903 In January, the Hotel Hollywood was opened on what was known as Prospect Avenue (now Hollywood Boulevard at Highland Avenue). It became the most important landmark in the city and a gathering place for movie people coming West.

1905   The Lubin Company's first studio in Philadelphia, a rooftop configuration for maximum daylight. Continuing to search for, among other things, better light, in a few years Lubin would open studios in New Mexico, Arizona and Hollywood.

1905 Prospect Avenue,
later renamed Hollywood
Boulevard.

*1905   Looking south onto
Hollywood from the hills.
In the foreground is one of
the city's still-preserved
landmarks now occupied
by the American Society of
Cinematographers.*

1905   The Delongpre estate on Cahuenga Avenue, home of French born painter, Paul deLongpre, becomes a top Hollywood tourist attraction.

COPYRIGHTED BY BYRON N.Y. 1906

THOMAS EDISON

A tribute from
Fuji Photo Film U.S.A., Inc.

1906   After developing moving pictures, Edison reflects upon an earlier invention, the phonograph. He had hoped the two technologies would be combined, but decided it was impractical.

41

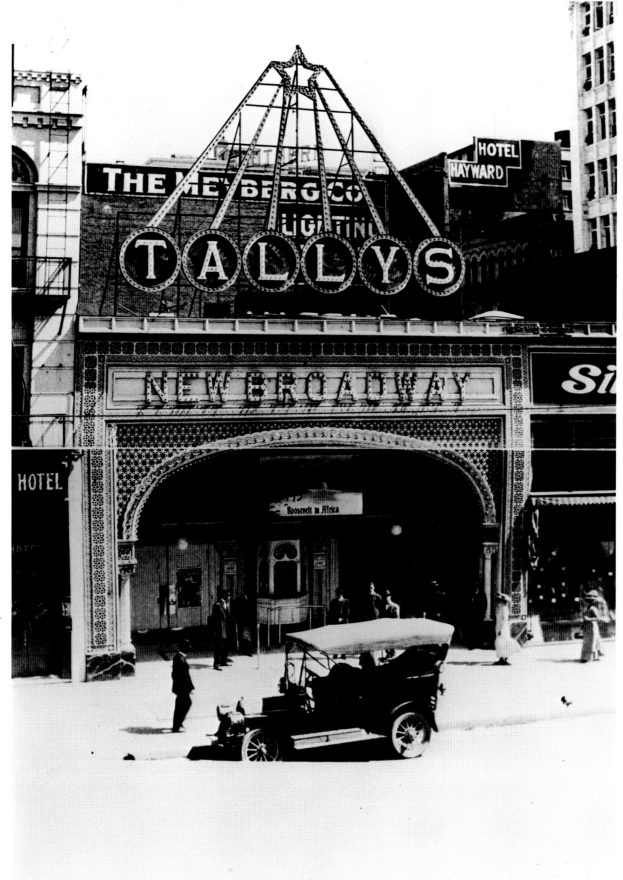

1906 Tally's New Broadway theater in downtown Los Angeles is known as the area's first real movie house.

ca. 1906   Hale's Tours, a successful novelty, sat audiences in passenger train seats and, using film projection, created the illusion of scenic train travel.

1907 The Selig Company from Chicago builds the first movie "set" in Los Angeles. The small stage for the film, "Carmen," was constructed over the skylights of a downtown building.

A tribute from
Peg Yorkin

*1907   A scene from
"Rescued from an Eagle's
Nest." This early Edison
film was written, directed
and photographed by
Edwin S. Porter and starred
D.W. Griffith, who would
later become a great film
director himself.*

3

The Third Decade 1907-1917

Moviemakers arrive in Southern California. They are welcomed by sedate residents with as much enthusiasm as the Goths and Vandals in ancient Rome. For the newcomers are mostly young and far from home; a rough, tough breed unfazed by physical hardship and disrespectful of private property. Denied entry to the better accommodations—"no dogs, no actors" read signs in family boarding houses and the Hollywood Hotel —they bunk together or camp out in the hills. To supplement primitive stages and painted flats, they shoot in the streets, drawing in passers-by as needed. Front lawns are no obstacle to real-life cowboys hired for the chase, and at day's end they let off steam by galloping through the streets, firing wildly.

Producer Mack Sennett covers street intersections with oil or soap to film the skids of unwary motorists; on one occasion provoking a nine-car pileup in a corner drug store. The aptly-named "Suicide" Lehrman, a former streetcar conductor, releases a lion among the crowd of volunteer extras to achieve a scene of panic. Other wild animals escape from menageries.

Productions are largely improvised, and are filmed quickly and cheaply by a director and cameraman, sometimes assisted by gag men, and by actors doubling as grips. There is little in the way of a scenario; producer Thomas Ince is ahead of his time in telling his directors to "shoot the script as written."

Pioneers build crude studios over an area of 300 square miles. The Santa Monica Mountains and Simi Valley are home to Indian villages and mining camps, in a fast replay of Western settlement and of the '49 Gold Rush. Unspoiled natural locations are a substantial asset; audiences are beginning to tire of seeing the landmarks of Fort Lee, N.J., in Westerns. Here it is still the Wild West. Rivals shoot it out in the tradition of the frontier, and boots are worn—not for effect, but to protect the wearers from rocks and rattlesnakes. Filming continues as long as it is light, six days a week.

The concentration of studios around the intersection of Sunset and Hollywood Boulevards and along Gower Street puts Hollywood at the center of the action. Though its residents initially refuse the honor, its name is soon shorthand for motion pictures. Director Alan Dwan, who arrives in 1912, later recalled: "We were beneath them. If we walked in streets with our cameras, they hid their girls under the beds, closed their doors and windows, and shied away." Two film companies threaten to move to "a town with more courtesy and consideration."

Glamour and profit prove stronger than moral principle. The star system creates instant celebrities, and fan magazines whip up public enthusiasm. Tourists come to stare. Carl Laemmle allows visitors to watch the action at his new studios in Universal City—and sells them eggs from his hatchery as they leave. Sons and daughters ignore parental warnings and the preachers' condemnations and dream of stardom.

Mae Marsh plays hooky from a Hollywood convent in 1910 to see her sister act in a D.W. Griffith picture. Two years later, she is working for him. In "The Real Tinsel," she recalls the experience: "Mr. Griffith would tell me exactly what to do. On the first day, he explained, 'I want you to sit on that rock wall over there. This boy you're sitting next to, you're very, very much in love with him. Have you ever been in love?' and I said, 'oh, yes!', which I hadn't. He said, 'Just think that you're terribly in love and look up at him, shy-like'. So I did, and then he said, 'Look up at him again and then put your head down', which I did. Then he said, 'Now get up and run away'. So I got up and ran away. That was my first acting part. I loved it. I said to Mr. Griffith, 'When am I going to do it again?' He said, 'You've done it once. You can't do it again. That was fine. Maybe you can do something else tomorrow.'" Mae Marsh goes on from this modest debut to star, unforgettably in *The Birth of a Nation* and *Intolerance*.

Movies prove hugely profitable. By 1915, the industry payroll is $20 million. Mae Marsh earns the standard $5 a day in her early years with Griffith. Mary Pickford goes from the same sum with Griffith in 1909 to $7000 a week in 1913 and the first million-dollar contract just three years later. Charlie Chaplin leaps from $150 a week in 1914 to $670,000 a year in 1916.

These astronomical salaries are justified by the productivity and drawing power of top stars. During his first year in the movies, 1914, Chaplin appears in a new picture almost every week, and wins instant recognition. "The sensation of the year," proclaims a trade paper, and exhibitors learn that they have only to put a picture of Chaplin on the sidewalk and announce, "He's here!," to sell out the house. Chaplin first realizes his potential worth on a train trip from Los Angeles to New York. Crowds line the track and throng the stations to wave. So great is the mob at New York's Grand Central Terminal that Chaplin is persuaded to alight at 125th Street and take an unobtrusive route to his hotel.

Directors are as responsive as producers and stars to the needs of their audience. D.W. Griffith makes over 400 short films for the Biograph Company, 1908-12, mostly in New York. With cameraman Billy Bitzer and a matchless stock company, he refines the art and technique of motion pictures, introducing subtleties of story telling and characterization, pictorial effects and editing, that rival the best European work. He inspires other professionals. Recalls Alan Dwan: "We just went down to the nickelodeon to see what Griffith was doing, and then we'd go out and do the same thing."

But the aspects of his work that are now most criticized and that will put an early end to his career in Hollywood—his Victorian sentimentality, his idealization of the child-woman, and his emphasis on such melodramatic themes as drunken husbands, infant mortality and destitute women—have strong appeal to the poor, immigrant audience for whom these are everyday problems. Other directors share these concerns, and though the audience is located in urban centers, its roots are in the countryside. Before the first World War, and even after, movies that show the triumph of small-town virtue over big city vice enjoy great popularity.

Hollywood is a small town that surrenders to the big city when, in 1910, it votes for annexation to Los Angeles in order to share another bonanza: the assured supply of water from the Owens Valley. Its population is now 4000, and empty lots are beginning to fill up with craftsman bungalows and elaborate mansions. (The Yamashiro Restaurant and the Magic Castle, above Franklin Avenue, are among the survivors.) A trolley runs up Laurel Canyon to a popular inn on Lookout Mountain. Yet, from the perspective of New York, it is still cut off. There is no telephone link to the East Coast until 1915, and the ritual four-day journey by train is the preferred way to go until 1950.

1907 The Kalem Company produces a ten-minute *Ben Hur* on a New York beach, with chariots borrowed from the 3rd Brooklyn Battery. The Chicago-based Selig Company completes its ten-minute *Count of Monte Cristo* on sets constructed behind a Chinese laundry in downtown Los Angeles, and on the La Jolla beach. It is the first professional movie to be shot in Southern California. The Chicago Police Department enforces local censorship ordinances. To avert other local initiatives, producers establish the National Board of Censorship (forerunner of today's National Board of Review) for self-regulation.

1908 Colonel Selig is the first to build a West-Coast movie studio, in Edendale (later, Echo Park). The first of 376 short Westerns starring "Bronco Billy" Anderson is filmed at Golden, Colorado.

1910 Kentucky-born D.W. Griffith, who hates the New York winters, makes his first trip to Southern California, where he directs numerous short dramas for Biograph.

Birth of the star system. Producer Carl Laemmle publicizes his signing of Florence Lawrence, formerly known as "the Biograph Girl." He leaks to the press a report that Lawrence is dead; then denounces this "cruel rumor" to build her up as "the IMP Girl." A public appearance and press conference in St. Louis follow. For a year or so, companies preserve the anonymity of their leading players, correctly anticipating that famous names will demand big increases in salary.

Top stage actors, including Geraldine Farrar and Herbert Beerbohm Tree, are persuaded to act before the cameras, to dignify the upstart medium with their renown. They are handsomely paid, but their performances on film prove inferior to those of actors who have grown up with the medium and understand its subtleties. Movie actors demand the same treatment as the failed luminaries of the theater. Independents willingly concede that a famous face is worth the price as a means of publicizing otherwise modest productions. Fan magazines soon appear, and run picture stories on the "private" lives of early stars.

1911 First Hollywood studio: the Nestor Company rents the Blondeau Tavern, closed by local temperance enthusiasts, at Sunset and Gower. (The site was taken over by Columbia Broadcasting System in 1938.) Producer Thomas Ince hires a Wild West Show for the winter, using the authentic cowboys and Indians, trained horses and buffalo, to make spectacular Westerns. This camp evolves into "Inceville," a 20,000-acre studio/ranch in Santa Ynez Canyon.

1912 Mack Sennett arrives in Los Angeles with his comedy troupe and (according to his own account) immediately exploits a Shriners' parade. Mabel Normand plays an unwed mother seeking help from the passing worthies, and Ford Sterling provokes a near riot. "God bless the Los Angeles Police," remarks Sennett, "they were the first Keystone Kops."

Adolph Zukor imports a prestigious French feature *Queen Elizabeth*, in an attempt to give motion pictures the prestige of legitimate theater, and to kill what he sees as the "slum tradition" in movies. The Warner brothers begin production; the Fox and Universal companies are founded.

Anita Loos, age 19, sells her first screenplay, *The New York Hat* to D.W. Griffith. He persuades her to write the titles for *Intolerance*, but her major achievement is to create a comic personality for the then young Douglas Fairbanks in a series of breezy satires directed by husband John Emerson. Later achievements include the novel, *Gentlemen Prefer Blondes*, which she adapts for the stage and screen, and the script for *San Francisco*.

1913   Cecil B. De Mille, sent to California by producers Jesse Lasky and Sam Goldwyn to film a stage Western, *The Squaw Man*, stopped in Arizona, but decides to continue on to Los Angeles. He rents half a horse barn at the junction of Selma and Vine, and (in early 1914) directs the first feature to be made in Hollywood proper.

It turns out to be a risky business. He is twice shot at, riding home through the Cahuenga Pass. His first negative is sabotaged; he takes to sleeping in the laboratory to protect the duplicate. He brings the picture in for a total budget of $15,450, and carries the print to New York. It has been wrongly perforated and cannot be projected. Siegmund Lubin, of Philadelphia, generously offers expert surgery. The film's success puts Hollywood on the map, encourages the migration of other eastern moviemakers, and launches the Lasky Feature Play Company, which will later become Paramount Pictures.

The still-surviving Regent in upper Manhattan is America's first movie palace, offering a standard of comfort and projection far in advance of the nickelodeons. Other movie palaces soon follow. A pioneer impresario is "Roxy" Rothafel, for whom the world's largest movie house will be named. "Don't give the public what they want," he insists, "Give them something better."

1914   Pearl White stars in a successful serial, *The Perils of Pauline*. Charlie Chaplin, a vaudeville performer hired off the stage by Sennett, invents the character of the Little Tramp, borrowing clothes and props from the company wardrobe. William S. Hart, a 44-year-old stage actor, who grew up in the West and speaks Sioux, applies for a job with Ince. "Bill, it's a damned shame," responds Ince. "The country has been flooded with Western pictures, they're a drug on the market." Hart ignores the advice, and goes on to become one of the most popular of Western stars, doing his own stunts and insisting on a gritty realism, as opposed to Hollywood glamour.

1915   D.W. Griffith's *The Birth of a Nation* stirs controversy. In his passion to convert Northerners to the Southern view of the Civil War and Reconstruction, he unwittingly sparks race riots and encourages the revival of the Ku Klux Klan. But President Wilson declares, "It is like writing history with lightning," following a private screening at the White House. *Birth* receives popular and critical acclaim, despite its racism, and gives motion pictures new status as an art and as a respectable form of entertainment.

William Fox plays Pygmalion to Theodosia Goodman, an unremarkable young woman from Cincinnati, whom he presents as Theda Bara, a man-eating vamp. Her debut in *A Fool There Was* creates a sensation; her phrase, "Kiss me, my Fool," gains wide currency. She goes on to play such vamp roles as Carmen, Cleopatra and Salome, but after five years audiences start to laugh and her career is effectively ended.

1916   Adolph Zukor creates the first motion picture conglomerate, merging his Famous Players company with Jesse Lasky's, and adding Paramount Pictures to handle distribution. He corners the top acting talent, and seeks block bookings on an annual roster of 104 features. Mary Pickford, "America's Sweetheart," is the chief lure to exhibitors, and to secure her exclusive services, Zukor makes her an offer she cannot refuse. According to Adela Rogers St. John, it comprises: $1,040,000 for two years' work, a bonus of $300,000 on signing, 50 percent of the profits, power to reject any picture of which she disapproves, exclusive use of a specially-constructed studio, a private rail car, two limousines, two maids, and her entire wardrobe on and off the screen. Two years later, Zukor is outbid by First National: Miss Pickford sweetly informs him that she simply cannot work for less than a million a year.

No less extravagant is Griffith's new feature, *Intolerance*, whose budget of $485,000 is 40 times that of a standard feature. The 150-ft. high set of Babylon towers over the cottages of East Hollywood, chariots can run along its walls, and shots are taken from a tethered balloon. Its masterly interweaving of four stories—the fall of Babylon, the persecution of Christ, the St. Bartholomew's Eve Massacre and a modern story of intolerance—remains one of the most ambitious projects ever undertaken in Hollywood, and serves as a model to Eisenstein and other great Soviet directors. But its complexities baffle contemporary audiences, and its message of brotherly love is at odds with the mood of the times.

*1908   The Selig Studio,
considered the first studio
in Los Angeles (as opposed
to Hollywood) was located
behind the Sing Loo
Chinese Laundry on Olive
Street between 7th and 8th.*

A tribute from
Bud Yorkin

1908 The Patents Company was an association of film company owners organized by Thomas Edison (foreground) for the purposes of licensing all independent film makers in the country. This, not surprisingly, was met with a great deal of resistance by these independents.

1910   Bison Film Company, Edendale (Echo Park district), was the second film company to come to California, arriving in 1909.

1911 This picture was taken on October 27, 1911, the first day of production for Hollywood's first motion picture studio. The converted Blondeau Tavern served as the Nestor Film Company's offices with filming of westerns and comedies in the rear.

1913 Universal City newly constructed in the Township of Lankershim.

5993

A tribute from
Daily Variety

*1913   Mack Sennet's
Keystone Cops in "In The
Clutches of The Law." Many
a Keystone star rose out of
the ranks of players, not
the least of whom was
Roscoe "Fatty" Arbuckle,
seen at the far right.*

1914   Inceville (today at Sunset Boulevard and Pacific Coast Highway). Thomas Ince, pioneer film producer/director for the Bison Film Company hired the Miller 101 Wild West Show composed entirely of authentic Sioux Indians.

A tribute from
Lorimar-Telepictures

1915 *Construction began
in September for Triangle
Studios, considered at the
time the showplace studio
of the West. The Triangle
Company consisted of
Thomas Ince, Mack Sennett
and D.W. Griffith, the most
important producers of the
time. The studios still stand
on Washington Blvd., in
Culver City, and recently
known as MGM, became
Lorimar Telepictures in 1986.*

1915 The Nestor Company of Bayonne, New Jersey, has established its Hollywood Studios at the northwest corner of Sunset Boulevard and Gower Street in 1911. Headed by David Horsley and Al Christie (far right) it becomes the first movie studio in Hollywood.

A tribute from
Eastman Kodak Company,
Motion Picture and
Audiovisual Products
Division

*1915 Mack Sennet direct-
ing dancer Dora Rogers in
a Keystone comedy, "Stolen
Magic," made under the
Triangle Company banner.*

ca. 1915   A Mack Sennet starlet illustrates how early costumes were designed to produce a sometimes startling effect.

1915 Lasky Feature Play Company studio, "The Barn," at the southeast corner of Selma and Vine Street in Hollywood. Stern's Barn was the site of Lasky Company's first feature film, "The Squaw Man," produced in December, 1913.

1916 Fred Kelsey directs a Universal western, "Love's Lariat," starring Harry Carey, on an open stage. Notice the Universal Studio Tour in the rear.

*1916   Universal City. Film
makers took advantage of
a rare snowfall to shoot
winter scenes.*

65

1916   D. W. Griffith's epic film, "Intolerance" was made entirely at the intersection of Hollywood and Sunset Boulevards. The sets stood 150 feet high and remained as a monument to the film for many years before they were taken down.

A tribute from
Hoffman Travel Service,
Inc., Carol Dunn-Tompkins

*1916   This photograph of
the "Intolerance" sets,
taken from the corner of
Prospect and Talmadge
Avenues, helps to illustrate
their enormous size.*

1916   A movie maker's view of what the old west was like, starring Harry Carey (second from left).

A tribute from
Filmland Corporate Center

*1916 A young producer,
Hal Roach (far left), and a
young comedian, Harold
Lloyd (in glasses) joined
forces in a movie debut
destined to start both on
the road to fame with the
"Lonesome Luke" series.*

ca. 1916   Early stars such
as Eileen Sedgwick, often
performed their own stunts.

A tribute from
Cesar Romero

*ca. 1916   Risky business,
but these sets built over a
Hill Street tunnel in
downtown Los Angeles
only enhanced the illusion
of perilous heights.*

is an image that will be echoed 25 years later by Gloria Swanson playing a faded silent star in *Sunset Boulevard.*

Chaplin is another kind of celebrity. Mobbed by fans in his earliest years, he becomes an increasingly private person, obsessed with his work, and laboring in his studio on La Brea Avenue to create a handful of lovingly polished movies. One short feature, *The Kid* takes 150 shooting days spread over two years, with cast and crew on full salary. For every foot of film used, 53 are developed. As his legend grows, he becomes ever more demanding of himself and his collaborators.

Europe continues to make films of outstanding artistic quality. *The Cabinet of Doctor Caligari,* a masterpiece of German expressionism, creates a stir. The costume epics of Ernst Lubitsch, *One Arabian Night* and *The Loves of Pharaoh,* inspire Fairbanks' historical spectacles; Mary Pickford invites Lubitsch to direct her in *Rosita.* That picture is withheld from release, but Lubitsch is launched on a dazzling, 25-year career in America. Hollywood buys up the finest talent: the first wave of immigrants gave birth to an industry, the second wave create an art. Maurice Tourneur is an early arrival from Paris. Victor Seastrom from Sweden, Paul Fejos from Hungary, Paul Leni and F.W. Murnau from Germany. All come to what another emigré, Josef von Sternberg, calls (in the opening title of *The Last Command),* "The Magic Empire of the Twentieth Century! The Mecca of the World!"

Resident artists are given extraordinary latitude, until the studios begin to assert tight budgetary control in the mid-twenties. Erich von Stroheim goes from playing "The Man You Love to Hate" in anti-German movies of the First World War, to the perverse but brilliant director of *Foolish Wives,* billed on Broadway as the first million-dollar production. He recreates the Monte Carlo Casino full-size beside the Los Angeles River, which stands in for the Mediterranean. For Samuel Goldwyn he adapts Frank Norris' brutally realistic novel *McTeague* and turns in *Greed,* which runs over eight hours in the director's cut. By now, the Goldwyn Company is a part of MGM, and Irving Thalberg, who earlier fired Stroheim from Universal, is its cost-efficient production head. *Greed* is cut to a quarter of its original length.

But Thalberg is willing to spend lavishly on productions that will increase the studio's standing and appeal to a broad audience. The production of *Ben Hur* in Italy is halted, and the picture is completed in Culver City, using miniatures in the studio tank for the naval battle, and constructing part of a stadium on open land to the south of Hollywood.

Buster Keaton is another free spirit who is unable to adjust to the studio system. The Woody Allen of the twenties, he creates a series of marvelously inventive, perfectly controlled comedies as an independent. Drawing on his vaudeville training he creates a character of balletic grace and stoic fortitude, who can master every threat, from a tornado to an abandoned ocean liner. Harold Lloyd plays a very different character, a brash striver whose cliffhanging comedy expresses the can-do spirit of the decade. *Safety Last* is a caricature of the theme of upwards mobility. Chaplin, Keaton and Lloyd are the best of those silent comedians whose art is fatally compromised by the coming of sound.

Hollywood is as big a contradiction as its movies. So great is its allure to young hopefuls, especially the "star-struck girl," that the Chamber of Commerce is driven to place ads in fan magazines warning that success eludes all but a few. Before Central Casting is established in 1926, extras are hired at the studio gate; frustration and hardship are rife. Cowboys hang out in "Gower Gulch" seeking work in the Westerns that are ground out by a hundred small companies along Poverty Row.

By contrast, this is the age of conspicuous consumption among the few who make it to the top. Mae Murray arrives at the studio in a Rolls Royce with *cloisonné* gold fittings, a sable rug across her lap. Clara Bow's convertible is painted to match her red hair and her chows. Gloria Swanson marries a French nobleman and cables Paramount: "Am arriving with the Marquis tomorrow. Please arrange ovation." A simpler life style survives amid the extravagance. Recalls character actor Paul Fix: "Hollywood was a beautiful little sleepy town...there was a restaurant at Cherokee called Armstrong & Carlton, and when you wanted to see movie stars, that's where you went."

The mansions along Hollywood Boulevard are replaced by movie palaces, hotels and restaurants, banks, agents' offices and fashionable stores, making it the Main Street of the movie colony. They are built in a variety of styles, as jumbled together as on any studio back lot. Pediments and fluted columns rub shoulders with Spanish arches and balconies, and with the zig zag ornament of art deco. Most exotic is Grauman's Chinese, which offers gala premieres, stage spectacles and the world's largest autograph album.

Some major studios move out of Hollywood in search of empty land, but smaller companies take over their lots. Chaplin faces his with a row of half-timbered English cottages (it is today the home of A&M Records). Bungalows house the army of craftsmen and spear-carriers. Luxury apartments disguised as Renaissance chateaus offer lodging to itinerant moviemakers; top stars and producers build Spanish haciendas and Tudor mansions in the hills. Frank Lloyd Wright creates innovative concrete-block houses for heiress Aileen Barnsdall and others. Hollywood's population rises to around 160,000 by the end of the decade.

1917 The U.S. enters the war against Germany; movies like *The Kaiser: The Beast of Berlin* amplify the jingoistic fervor that sweeps the nation. Jesse Lasky forms a home guard from studio employees, and drills them with prop rifles. Warner Bros. makes its mark with *My Four Years in Germany*, which is shot in New Jersey but claims to show authentic pictures of the brutal Hun.

An exhibitors' association, First National, becomes a major force in production, buying talent and distributing independent work.

1918 Top stars draw huge crowds to war bond rallies. D.W. Griffith's *Hearts of the World* and Chaplin's *Shoulder Arms* bring a rare artistry to the subject of war.

1919 Chaplin, Pickford, Fairbanks and Griffith form United Artists, to distribute their own productions. The move is inspired by an awareness of their own popularity, and to maintain artistic control in the face of a rumored consolidation of major producers. "The lunatics have taken over the asylum," scoffs an industry executive. The American Society of Cinematographers is established.

1920 *The Four Horsemen of the Apocalypse* makes Rudolph Valentino a major star. Louis B. Mayer produces *Sinners in Silk*, "whose slogan is speed and whose hymn is jazz," an early entry in the "flaming youth" sweepstakes.

1921 Fatty Arbuckle, the corpulent comedian whose popularity rivals Chaplin's, is accused of murdering actress Virginia Rappe during a drunken weekend party at a San Francisco hotel. Arbuckle is acquitted of the charge by a jury ("We feel a great injustice has been done to him"), but the press has destroyed his reputation in a series of inflammatory headlines. His films are withdrawn, his career is ended. Industry leaders hire the Postmaster-General, Will Hays, to "clean up Hollywood."

The first concerts are held in the Hollywood Bowl, formerly known as "Daisy Dell." Russian-born actress Alla Nazimova opens the Garden of Allah hotel on Sunset Strip. It is to become a favorite resort for writers, from Robert Benchley to Scott Fitzgerald. Alexander Woolcott will later describe it as, "the kind of village you might look for down a rabbit hole."

The Motion Picture Relief Fund, now known as the Motion Picture and Television Fund, is founded by Mary Pickford, Charlie Chaplin, Douglas Fairbanks and other industry pioneers.

1922 Fairbanks' *Robin Hood* runs six months as the opening attraction at Grauman's Egyptian Theater.

An anonymous pamphlet, *The Sins of Hollywood,* declares that: "There is something about the pictures which seems to make men and women less human and more animal-like."

1923 Wallace Reid, a popular actor, dies of morphine addiction. His wife Dorothy Davenport stars in *Human Wreckage,* which warns that: "Dope is the gravest menace which today confronts the United States. Immense quantities of morphine, heroin and cocaine are yearly smuggled into America."

De Mille's *The Ten Commandments,* recreates ancient Egypt in the California desert. (Excavations are currently in progress to recover the buried ruins.) Another epic, *The Covered Wagon,* chronicles the trek West, using authentic locations and wagons.

1924 Metro-Goldwyn-Mayer established by Loew's Inc., the New York-based theater chain. Louis B. Mayer will head the studio for the next 27 years. Columbia Pictures begins its long struggle towards the major league under the leadership of Harry Cohn.

William Cameron Menzies launches his career as the first production designer by creating the enormous art nouveau palace for Fairbanks' *The Thief of Bagdad.*

1925 Swedish starlet Greta Garbo arrives in Hollywood with her favorite director, Mauritz Stiller. MGM is uncertain how to exploit its prize, putting Garbo in running shorts and posing her with the USC track team for publicity photographs.

King Vidor directs *The Big Parade,* an impassioned portrait of the ordinary American caught up in war. It makes a star of John Gilbert.

1926 Ten million American families have radios, and the audience begins to stay home to listen to favorite entertainers. Warner Bros. experiments with sound and releases *Don Juan* with synchronized music on disc.

1919 "Inceville." Established in 1911 in Santa Ynez Canyon, at the foot of Sunset Boulevard and Pacific Coast Highway. Here pioneer director Thomas Ince made many films with such stars as William S. Hart and Sessue Hayakawa.

A tribute from
Walter Shenson

*1921   On the Willat Studio
back lot on Washington
Blvd. in Culver City,
designer/builder Edwin
Willat (brother of the studio
owner and director, Irvin
Willat) supervises the
"country mansion"
miniature, built for the film
"Face of the World." A
dramatic episode in the
film featured the burning of
the set.*

1921   This unusually candid picture illustrates a studio photographer's infatuation with the youthful beauty of Mary Pickford.

A tribute from
Mary Pickford Foundation

ca. 1921   Mack Sennet players illustrate the kind of camaraderie early studios nurtured.

1923 Lunchbreak on the set of Paramount's "The Ten Commandments" produced and directed by Cecil B. DeMille.

A tribute from
Joe Hamilton
Productions, Inc.

*1923 The original Holly-
wood sign just after com-
pletion. It was built for a
real estate development.
During World War II, the
"land" section of the sign fell
down, leaving the city with
it s now famous landmark.*

1923 Highly stylized costume design from Alla Nazimova production of "Salome." Nazimova was a legendary star of the silent era, as well as a producer, director, designer and writer of films. In the late 1920's, she transformed her estate into an apartment/hotel complex known as "The Garden of Alla."

*1924   Will Rogers (left) and
Hal Roach on the polo field of
Roach's ranch in Culver City.*

1925 Universal Studios founder and president, Carl Laemmle, (fifth from right) and his son, Carl, Jr. (third from right) wait their turn for paychecks with other studio employees such as Jean Hersholt (third from left). A tongue-in-cheek photograph, however it does clearly show the emphasis the studios placed upon a "family" working environment.

*1925   Greta Garbo arrives
in America in the summer
of 1925. With her is her
director and mentor,
Mauritz Stiller, (left) who
discovered Garbo at the
Stockholm Royal Dramatic
Theater.*

1926 The marriage of May Murray and Prince Mdivani (center) was an important media event in which Hollywood became the center of international attention. Such European stars as Rudolph Valentino and Pola Negri, (far right) not only attended, but were best man and woman.

A tribute from
Ellis Mercantile Company

1927 Gary Cooper (center) during shooting of "Nevada," one of his first important film roles. While on location, stars and technicians both worked together and lunched together.

*1927 There's probably a
good reason for Jack
Warner and Al Jolson
(right) to be in such a good
mood. That year's release
of "The Jazz Singer" revi-
talized Warner Bros. studios
and began the sound era.
Warner Bros. had gambled
a great deal of money retro-
fitting theaters with sound
equipment. The success of
"The Jazz Singer" paid off.*

th

R

JOLSON.PUB.Y.

A tribute from
The Hollywood Reporter

*1927   Fanny Brice arrives
in Hollywood at the invita-
tion of Darryl F. Zanuck
(seen right) to debut in her
first film, "My Man." With
her is the film's skillful
director Archie Mayo.*

5

The Fifth Decade 1927-1937

The success of *The Jazz Singer,* a silent picture, enhanced with Al Jolson's songs and a few lines of improvised dialogue, takes Hollywood by surprise. Edison had experimented with synchronized sound; inventor Lee De Forest had demonstrated talkies in the mid-twenties. But the major studios see it as a highly disruptive and unnecessary change. Their contract players, stages and theaters are all geared to a well-proven system. The silent film has achieved great expressive power; live musical accompaniment and sound effects compensate for the lack of dialogue.

A Fox sound newsreel of Lindbergh's departure for Paris in January 1927 fails to persuade the skeptics. But Warner Bros. is not yet a major studio. Heavy investment from Wall Street has given it the potential to become one, but it has no access to first-run theaters; it must gamble or starve to death. *Don Juan* is a first step, but the movies already have live music. What radio has, and movies lack, is speech. Jolson has a huge following, and the simplicity of his first line, "You ain't heard nothing yet," is enough. Crowds besiege the few theaters that are wired for sound, following the New York premiere in October 1927.

Warner Bros. announces that it is making 12 more talkies; Fox follows suit. Other studios pray the fad will pass. But audiences steadily grow. By summer of 1928, 300 theaters are equipped. The majors scurry to catch up, and for a year all is chaos. Actors are the critical element; will they record? No one has ever had to learn lines or perform on a silent stage before. In the immortal words of Gloria Swanson in "Sunset Boulevard": "They had the eyes of the whole world but that wasn't enough ...so they opened their big mouths, and out came talk! Talk! Talk!"

Some actors leave right away; they include Norma Talmadge ("Thank God mother established the trust fund!"), Colleen Moore, Pola Negri, and Emil Academy give him his Oscar before he leaves). Others later wished they had. The most celebrated failure is John Gilbert, who insists on serving out his four-year, million-dollar contract with MGM, and is utterly humiliated. King Vidor maintains that his voice was fine, and that his style as a silent lover adapted badly to the new conventions of sound. For different reasons, Clara Bow and Rin Tin Tin are among the casualties.

The sound engineer is king, deciding which voices will record and which will fail; imprisoning the cameraman in a suffocating, sound-proofed box, and tying down actors to the spot where the microphone is hidden. Audiences are sorely tested as Hollywood tries to master new techniques, train new talent and build sound-proofed stages. "All talking, all singing, all *terrible,*" sneers a *grande dame* of the stage in *The Royal Family of Broadway,* and movie connoisseurs feel the same way. But the techniques are mastered, thanks to such innovative directors as Rouben Mamoulian; attendance shoots up, new genres are born, and the camera recovers its freedom of motion.

It is a golden opportunity for writers, and they flock in, from the Algonquin in New York and the newsrooms of Chicago. Herman Mankiewicz is an early arrival and he summons another alumnus of the *Chicago Tribune* with a telegram: "Will you accept three hundred per week to work for Paramount Pictures. All expenses paid. The three hundred is peanuts. Millions are to be grabbed out here and your only competition is idiots. Don't let this get around." In his autobiography, *"A Child of the Century,"* Ben Hecht boasts: "For many years, Hollywood held this double lure for me, tremendous sums of money for work that required no more effort than a game of pinochle. Of the sixty movies I wrote, more than half were written in two weeks or less."

Hecht's credits include *The Front Page, Twentieth Century* and much of *Gone with the Wind.* Lesser talents have a harder time. Jack Warner dubs his contract writers, "Schmucks with Underwoods" and insists they clock in and out. Writers are reported to have been compelled to submit 11 pages every Thursday or be fired. Literary geniuses, including William Faulkner, Scott Fitzgerald and Nathanael West are driven, by a lack of royalties, to screenwriting. "A mining camp in lotus land" is how Fitzgerald sees the town, and West's *The Day of the Locust* is a pitiless exposé.

Sound rescues the movies from a triple threat: declining audiences, the competition of radio and television, and the impact of the Depression. Booming fortunes insulate Hollywood from the immediate impact of the Stock Market Crash in November, 1929. Had the crash come two years sooner the banks would not have been able to fund the change-over, the studios (and their theater chains) might not have ridden out the storm. Even so, it is a close call. By 1932, four of the eight major studios in Hollywood are facing bankruptcy and a third of the nation's theaters are shuttered. Layoffs and pay cuts pull the studios through. Double-bills and dish-nights help lure the audiences back to the theaters.

Desperation stalks the land. A quarter of the nation's work force is unemployed. Banks and businesses are tottering. Hollywood captures the frenzy, then raises morale. The best movies of 1931-33 have a sense of urgency and excitement never matched before or since. The Production Code, introduced in 1930, is set aside. In 1931 alone, 50 gangster pictures are produced, including *Little Caesar, Public Enemy*—and *Scarface*, which Ben Hecht bases on the life of Al Capone. Its violence shocks many, and it is finally released with the subtitle "The Shame of a Nation," and a printed warning: "This is an indictment against gang rule in America and the careless indifference of the government...What are you going to do about it?"

Frank Capra's *American Madness* castigates the complacency of bankers; *Gabriel over the White House* hints that a fascist system of government might work better than the present muddle. Warner Bros. specializes in movies whose themes are "torn from the headlines". *I am a Fugitive from a Chain Gang* exposes the cruelty of the penal system and prompts reform; *Heroes for Sale* denounces public indifference towards war veterans—a theme that is echoed by the "My Forgotten Man" number in a back-stage musical, *Golddiggers of 1933*. The movies and real life constantly intersect. John Dillinger, the FBI's Most-Wanted fugitive, is shot dead by G-men leaving a movie house. He is "nuts about Clark Gable" and has been watching his hero play a gangster on Death Row.

America regains its confidence with the election of Roosevelt and the proclamation of the New Deal. Hollywood responds to the sharp shift in the public temper. Gangsters and their molls are out, glinty-eyed G-men and wholesome heroes are in. Shirley Temple displaces Mae West as top box-office attraction, and holds her lead for four years. Censorship is tightly enforced, and movies insist that crime does not pay, and that even married couples sleep in separate beds.

Frank Capra creates a world of honest underdogs outsmarting crooks and fixers, entertaining even as he slips in the message that guts and principle will carry you through hard times. Capra is an immigrant, from Sicily, whose own life is a Horatio Alger tale. With the zeal of a con-vert, he creates archetypal American heroes: Mr. Deeds and Mr. Smith are still held up as models. Walt Disney's mythic heroes prove equally durable. Cartoons prove as encouraging as Capra's fables, and they offer the precious gift of laughter. Screwball comedies lampoon the rich and extol the poor, defusing resentment at the gaping inequalities of contemporary life

The Depression continues through the decade and, for most Americans, the movies offer the only affordable escape. An ad in the *Saturday Evening Post* says it all: "Go to a motion picture! Before you know it you are living the story—laughing, loving, hating, struggling, winning. All the adventure, all the romance, all the excitement you lack in your daily life are in—Pictures! They take you out of yourself, out of the cage of daily existence."

Each studio has its own style, expressed in its choice of stories, actors and visuals. MGM is opulent and escapist. Its Supervising Art Director, Cedric Gibbons, is the high priest of white-on-white decor, and in the pictures he oversees every secretary has her deco penthouse. Adrian dresses Garbo and Norma Shearer, Joan Crawford and Jean Harlow, and has a greater impact on what American women wear than all the couturiers of Paris. "Garbo's hats are like fashion Fords", he remarks. Pro-duction Chief Irving Thalberg personally supervises such prestige pictures as *The Merry Widow, Mutiny on the Bounty, Romeo and Juliet* and *The Good Earth,* from inception to release, re-shooting and re-editing to achieve a high polish.

Warner Bros. rivals MGM in profitability, but it follows a different course. Its chief art director, Polish-born Anton Grot, is constantly frustrated in his attempts to create grandiose sets, though he has his fling in the Max Reinhardt production, *A Midsummer Night's Dream.* Busby Berkeley's kaleidoscopic dance numbers dazzle the eye, but Warners' strong suit is earthy realism. Its writers, actors and crews are driven hard, grinding out pictures, back to back. Jack Warner, Darryl Zanuck and Hal Wallis set the pace; Bette Davis and Jimmy Cagney, Edward G. Robinson and Errol Flynn respond—with electric energy and a refreshing sense of the times.

The coming of sound drives moviemakers indoors, to achieve the technical and budgetary control of the stage and the back lot. Hollywood changes. The stars who had earlier lived, shopped and lunched in Hollywood now appear only after dark, to be seen at gala premieres or in the nightclubs on Sunset Strip. William De Mille, who had joined his brother Cecil in the earliest years and had made his own reputation as a director, bemoans the changes wrought by sound: "Within two years our little old Hollywood was gone, and in its place stood a fair new city, talking a new language, having different manners and customs; a more terrifying city, full of strange faces, less friendly, more businesslike, twice as populous —and much more cruel."

1927 "Suggestive films and ultra sex films have become altogether too numerous of late," complains William Randolph Hearst.

F.W. Murnau's *Sunrise* and Buster Keaton's *The General* exemplify the artistry of silent cinema, doomed by the talkie revolution.

The Academy of Motion Picture Arts and Sciences is founded.

1928 King Vidor caps his career at MGM by directing three silent pictures in a year: *The Patsy* and *Show People* demonstrate Marion Davies' neglected gifts as a comedienne; *The Crowd* is a harrowing portrayal of a man crushed by fortune in New York City, starring an unknown who will never act again.

Mickey Mouse makes his debut in Disney's *Steamboat Willie.*

1929 The first Academy Awards dinner is held in May at the Hollywood Roosevelt Hotel. Douglas Fairbanks presents the Oscars in just five minutes. *Wings* is judged Best Picture starring a handsome juvenile named Charles "Buddy" Rogers; Frank Borzage wins the Best Director award for *Seventh Heaven;* Emil Jannings and Janet Gaynor are given Oscars for Best Actor and Actress. All the major awards are to silent pictures; for the only time, an award is given for best title writing.

Rouben Mamoulian's debut, *Applause,* is shot at Paramount's Astoria Studios in New York. Mamoulian ignores the advice of the sound engineers and brings a new sophistication to the fledgling technology. The Marx Brothers also make their screen debut at Astoria, filming *Cocoanuts* during the day, and performing on stage in the evening.

1930 The popularity of sound boosts theater attendance to a record high of 100 million a week. Garbo talks—in *Anna Christie.* Lewis Milestone directs a powerful adaptation of Erich Maria Remarque's *All Quiet on the Western Front* for Carl Laemmle at Universal, shooting the picture silent and post-dubbing the sound. Marie Dressler and Wallace Beery star in a surprise hit, *Min and Bill,* a film that defies the MGM tradition of glamor. Paramount's newest star is Marlene Dietrich, who appears in the German-made *The Blue Angel,* and co-stars with Gary Cooper in *Morocco.*

William Fox, one of the top moguls of the silent era, is wiped out by the stock-market crash, and is forced to sell his studio.

First experimental television transmissions are beamed from New York's station W2XBS (later WNBC).

There are two Academy Awards ceremonies in one year, the first in April, the second in November, both at the Ambassador Hotel, both broadcast by a local radio station.

1931 CBS inaugurates the first regular television service in New York, broadcasting for seven hours a day.

Clark Gable makes his mark in a Joan Crawford vehicle, *Dance, Fools, Dance,* and appears in 11 other pictures released in this one year. Bela Lugosi, the star of *Dracula,* turns down the leading role in *Frankenstein,* which makes the reputation of Boris Karloff.

1932 Ernst Lubitsch crowns a decade of sophisticated comedies, made at Warner Bros. and then at Paramount, with *Trouble in Paradise.* The "Lubitsch Touch" is widely admired, but seldom matched.

Fredric March (*Dr. Jekyll and Mr. Hyde*) and Wallace Beery (*Grand Hotel*) share the Academy Award for Best Actor.

1933 The Screen Actors' Guild and the Screen Writers' Guild are established.

RKO is planning a lost-world picture, *Creation.* Producer-director Merian C. Cooper reports to David O. Selznick: "The present story construction and the use of the animals is entirely wrong...I suggest a prehistoric Giant Gorilla, fifty times as strong as a man—a creature of nightmare horror and drama." The result is, *King Kong.* Recalls actress Fay Wray: "Producers promised me the tallest, darkest leading man in Hollywood. I thought of Gable and when the script came, I was appalled. I thought it was a practical joke."

Also at RKO, Fred Astaire and Ginger Rogers appear in *Flying Down to Rio.* Within a year they have top billing, and appear in a succession of elegant, witty dance musicals.

1934 The Legion of Decency is established by Catholic laymen to compel Hollywood to enforce its Production Code—announced in 1930 to guarantee on-screen morality, but then ignored.

Writer-producer Darryl Zanuck becomes Production Head of newly-formed Twentieth Century-Fox.

1935 *Becky Sharp* is the first full Technicolor feature. *It Happened One Night,* a sleeper, wins the top five Oscars for Columbia Pictures.

1936 The Screen Directors Guild is established.

Chaplin continues to defy convention by making *Modern Times* with almost no dialogue.

Fritz Lang, one of many refugees from Nazi Germany, expresses his hatred of mob rule in *Fury.*

The death of Irving Thalberg, MGM's production chief, at age 37.

*1930 The Hal Roach
Studio, "Our Gang" kids
take a school break with
their teacher Fern Carter,
during the filming of
"Shivering Shakespeare."*

A tribute from Paramount Pictures Corporation

1930 Hollywood extras soon learn when a big picture is going into production. Here's a casting call for 500 bearded miners for Paramount's production of "The Spoilers," starring Gary Cooper

1930   William S. Hart (right) returns to the western set as an actor and technical advisor to director King Vidor (center) and Johnny Mack Brown (left) during the filming of "Billy The Kid."

A tribute from
Foto-Kem Motion Picture
and Video Tape Laboratory

*ca. 1930   Universal Studios
receives a distinguished
visitor, Dr. Albert Einstein,
seen here talking to Universal founder and president,
Carl Laemmle.*

1930 At the Goldwyn Studios, dance director Busby Berkeley lines up a shot for the film, "Whoopie," starring Eddie Cantor.

104

A tribute from
Sharon Gless

*ca. 1932   Young Paramount
stars Carole Lombard and
Clark Gable on a lunch
break at the commissary.
MGM loaned Gable to
Paramount to work with
Lombard.*

ca. 1934 At the RKO Studio, Fred Astaire takes time to sign autographs for his fans.

A tribute from
Coldwater Canyon Lawn
Tennis Association

*ca. 1934   Harvey Snodgrass,
tennis pro at the Beverly
Hills Hotel, instructs MGM
star, Jean Harlow.*

ca. 1934 One of Claudette Colbert's most important roles and one of DeMille's best costume epics, "Cleopatra."

A tribute from
Michael J. Fox

*ca. 1935 James Cagney's
tough guy reputation didn't
necessarily come from
press releases. Shown here
with instructor Harvey Parry.*

ca. 1935 People who make other people happy enjoy a moment for themselves. Stan Laurel, Walt Disney and Oliver Hardy.

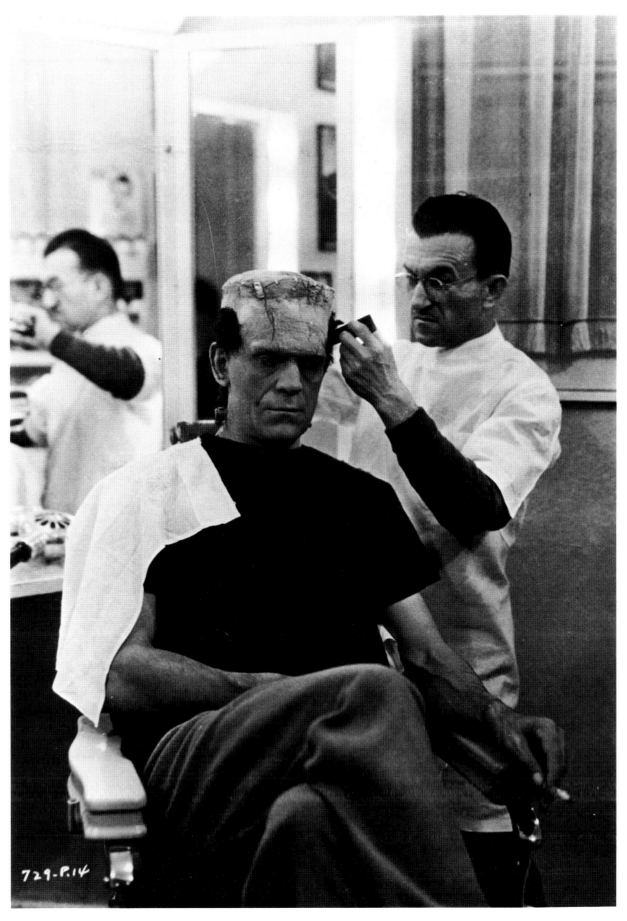

729-P.14

*1935   At Universal Studios,
Jack Pierce, makeup
department chief, trims
Boris Karloff during the
shooting of "Bride of
Frankenstein."*

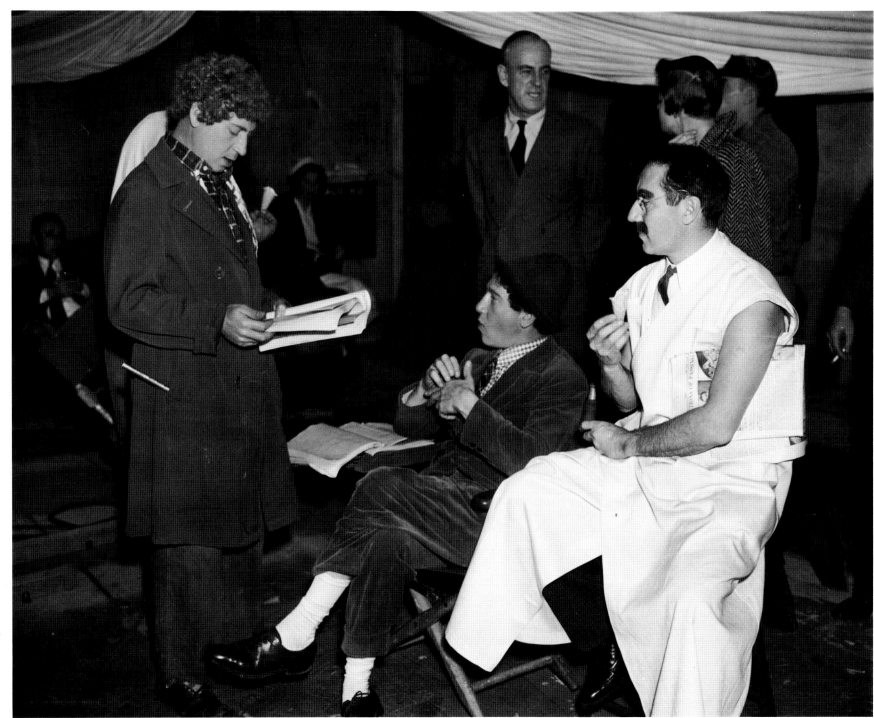

1935 The Marx Brothers study a script between takes for "A Day At The Circus" (MGM). Note that Harpo is reading the lines to his brothers.

A tribute from
Bernard Schwartz

*ca. 1935   Producer Howard
Hughes supervised the
shooting of aerial scenes
for "Sky Devils."*

*ca. 1936   Bing Crosby
starts a trend in bicycle
riding at Paramount Studios.*

A tribute from
Fries Entertainment, Inc.

*ca. 1937   Spencer Tracy
and his favorite horse,
"Two Socks" at his favorite
sport.*

ca. 1937 W.C. Fields in front of his beach house. The photo says it all.

A tribute from
AFTRA—American
Federation of Television
and Radio Artists

*1937   Three comediennes
who appear in Paramount's
"College Swing," left to right,
Cecile Cunningham, Gracie
Allen and Martha Raye.*

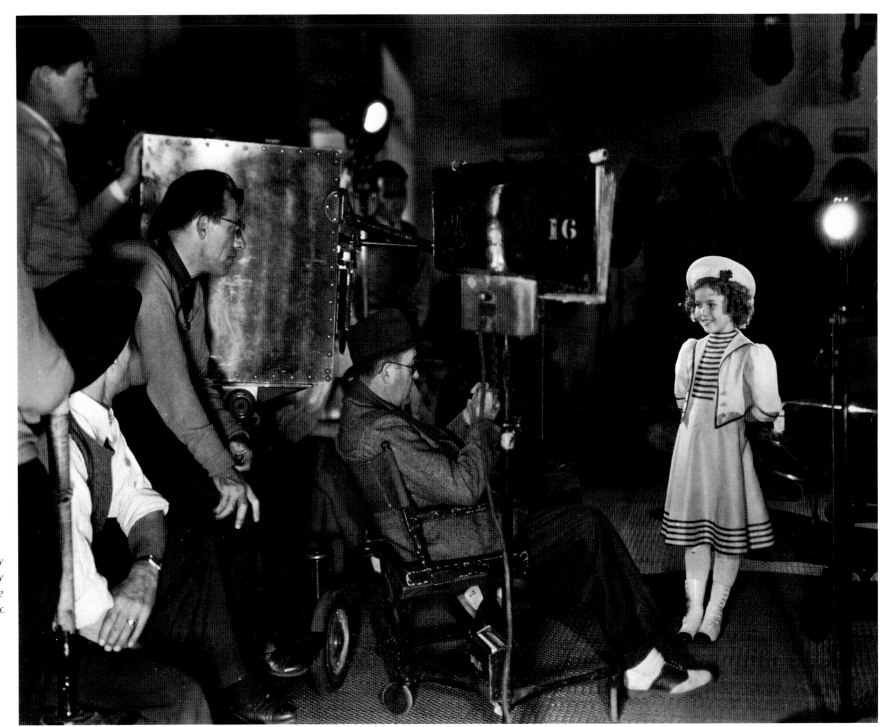

1937   John Ford directs by now veteran star, Shirley Temple, in 'Wee Willie Winkie" at 20th Century Fox.

A tribute from
Ralph Bellamy

1937   Director Frank Capra takes a break with his stars Sam Jaffe and Ronald Colman at the door of the Columbia studios production of "Lost Horizon."

6

The Sixth Decade 1937-1947

By general consent, the late thirties and early forties mark the peak of the studio system: the years in which art, craft and popular appeal are most successfully combined. The industry runs with a smoothness that present-day tycoons must envy. Almost every major talent and an army of skilled supporters are under contract, ready to accept any assignment or to be loaned out to another studio. There are fluctuations in attendance, but theaters steadily recover from Depression blues, and admissions boom when war removes other distractions.

The peak year for all-around excellence is 1939. *Gone With the Wind* takes eight Oscars against stiff competition. Also released that year are: *Gunga Din, Mr. Smith Goes to Washington, Ninotchka, Only Angels have Wings, Stagecoach, The Wizard of Oz, The Women, Wuthering Heights* and *Young Mr. Lincoln.*

Contributing to this surge of great entertainment are famous faces on screen and less familiar names behind the camera. No cinematographer advances the art more than Gregg Toland. His dramatic lighting on *Wuthering Heights* and his deep-focus photography on *Citizen Kane* and *The Best Years of Our Lives* demonstrate his range. But he is also the master of naturalism in *The Grapes of Wrath,* and he co-directs a war documentary, *December 7th* with John Ford. A stylist, who brings something of himself to every film he shoots in this decade, he dies at age 44 in 1948.

Hollywood's meteoric success during this period is not Orson Welles, whose impatient genius makes him too many enemies, but Preston Sturges. The son of socialites, and the inventor of a kiss-proof lipstick, he writes and directs seven of the best movie satires in just five years. Nothing is sacred: hero worship and patriotism are lampooned as pointedly as corrupt politicians, advertising mythology and sex. Among the highlights are Barbara Stanwyck's courtship of Henry Fonda in *The Lady Eve*; the send-up of social realism as Joel McCrea seeks a higher truth in *Sullivan's Travels*; and Claudette Colbert among the millionaires in *Palm Beach Story.*

There are more stars than even MGM's heaven can contain. Katharine Hepburn, denounced as "box-office poison" in an exhibitor's poll, recovers her place at the top in a dazzling sequence of starring roles: *Bringing Up Baby, Holiday, The Philadelphia Story* and *Woman of the Year.* She shares the first three of these with Cary Grant, who ranges even wider with his role as editor Walter Burns in Howard Hawks' *His Girl Friday,* a cockney subaltern in George Stevens' *Gunga Din,* and a suave spy in Alfred Hitchcock's *Notorious.* Garbo laughs in *Ninotchka* and Marlene Dietrich makes a great comeback, co-starring with Jimmy Stewart in the bawdy Western, *Destry Rides Again.*

The finest musical talents of Europe are in Hollywood, from choice or necessity. Irving Thalberg invites Arnold Schoenberg to compose the score for *The Good Earth*; the master agrees to do so if he is allowed to direct the actors so that they read their lines in the right key. MGM declines this favor, but the following year Schoenberg gets to present the Oscar for best musical score—to Charles Previn, head of the Universal Music Department, for *A Hundred Men and a Girl.* Hungarian-born Miklos Rozsa wins his first Oscar for *Spellbound.* Czech prodigy Erich Wolfgang Korngold, pronounced a genius by Puccini, stirs the blood with his brazen scores for the Errol Flynn swashbucklers. Viennese Max Steiner arrives with the talkies and scores many of Hollywood's finest pictures, from *King Kong* to *Casablanca,* from *Gone With the Wind* to *The Treasure of the Sierra Madre.*

Even the much-maligned moguls have their fans. Says Katharine Hepburn of Louis B. Mayer: "He adored the business and he understood it. I truly admired him, and Sam Goldwyn, and Harry Cohn and all those birds. They made the industry what it is...or was. It never would have existed without them." And Frank Capra, who made his best pictures for Harry Cohn at Columbia, said (in "The Men Who Made the Movies"): "He ran his own place. He didn't have a committee running it. Not even the people from New York would tell him what to do, and so he made his own decisions, and it's wonderful to be working for a man who can give you a yes or a no right now, and mean it, and not go back on it."

Unlike other industries, Hollywood is prepared for war. It has no need to retool. It has rehearsed its mission, to entertain and boost morale, to strengthen resolve and codify national myths, throughout the Depres-

*1937   Eddie Albert in an
early NBC Television
Production.*

A tribute from
AT&T

*ca. 1937   Stuntman Otto
Mazzeti, brother of famed
actor/stuntman Richard
Talmadge, at the Columbia
Ranch in Burbank.*

ca. 1937   A candid look at Charlie Chaplin with his famous bride, Paulette Goddard.

*ca. 1937 Jerry Howard,
Moe Howard and Larry
Fine, The Three Stooges,
at the Columbia Ranch in
Burbank.*

1938 Norma Shearer and Tyrone Power at a time when Hollywood premieres were the most glamorous. Here, at the opening of "Marie Antoinette," at the Fox Carthay Circle Los Angeles, witnessed by 25,000 wide-eyed fans.

A tribute from
Amblin Entertainment

1939   On the set of "Gone With the Wind." Left to right: Vivian Leigh, Clark Gable and director Victor Fleming, along with the film's script supervisor.

1939 Mr. and Mrs. Jim Jordan (Fibber McGee and Molly), Charlie McCarthy and Edgar Bergen sign at RKO Pictures for the film "Charlie McCarthy, Detective."

A tribute from
James Stewart

1939 James Stewart watches the spectacular parade scenes which climax "Mr. Smith Goes to Washington." The Columbia Pictures' classic was directed by Frank Capra, second from right.

1940 Buster Keaton shows Jeannette MacDonald a rare piece of embroidery done by his mother. The two were making an MGM film, "New Moon," with Nelson Eddy.

A tribute from
Angie Dickinson

*1941   Ronald Reagan and
Nancy Coleman in Warner
Bros.' "Kings Row," with
Ann Sheridan and Robert
Cummings.*

1941   A night scene at Wrigley Field Stadium with several thousand extras taking part in Frank Capra's "Meet John Doe," a Warner Bros. picture starring Gary Cooper.

A tribute from
Bobrow/Thomas & Assoc.

*1941 A ground-breaking
at the Motion Picture and
Television Country House
in Woodland Hills,
California.*

1941 Bud Abbott and Lou Costello (on boom at upper left) during filming of "Ride 'Em Cowboy" at Universal Pictures.

A tribute from
Ginnie and Bob Newhart

*1942   Lieutenant Colonel
Nelson inspects Clark
Gable's M-1 at Boot Camp.
Gable joined the Air Force
in 1942 after the tragic
death of his wife Carole
Lombard. She was killed in
an airplane crash while on
a War Bond Drive. Gable
achieved the rank of Major
and received the Distin-
guished Flying Cross and
Air Medal for flying several
bombing missions over
Germany*

1942   Director Ernst Lubitsch with his newest star, Jack Benny, working over a scene from "To Be Or Not To Be." Benny played opposite Carole Lombard in her last film before her death.

A tribute from
3-M Professional Audio and
Video Products

1946 A general industry strike, with intermittent violence, affects many Hollywood studios including Warner Bros., shown here.

ca. 1946 George Jessel is surrounded by pals at a Friar's Club dinner. Seated: Jack Benny, George Jessel, and L. B. Mayer; Standing: Danny Kaye, Pat O'Brian, Bob Hope and Al Jolson.

A tribute from
Batjac Productions, Inc.

1946   Happy 30th, Rita!
Errol Flynn, Nora Edding-
ton Flynn, Rita Hayworth
and Orson Welles, October
17. Photographed on Flynn's
boat during the filming of
"Lady from Shanghai."

ca. 1946   Jimmy Durante
and Frank Sinatra with TV
star Garry Moore at CBS
Hollywood.

ca. 1947   An unusual location shot of Bogart and Bacall on the set of "Key Largo," Warner Bros.

7

The Seventh Decade 1947-1957

Like the biblical plagues in a Cecil B. De Mille epic, troubles rain down on Hollywood. Strikes, trade disputes, anti-trust action, a flight of the audience to suburbia, witchhunts and television combine to destroy an edifice 50 years in the making.

Even before the end of the Pacific war, the studios are hit with a prolonged and violent strike. Britain, which is Hollywood's chief overseas market, clamps a 75 percent tax on the earnings of imported pictures; Hollywood responds with an extended boycott. The U.S. Department of Justice resumes an anti-trust suit, first brought before the war, which seeks to compel studios to surrender their theater chains, and thus lose a captive market for their movies.

Most damaging to morale are the charges of disloyalty. Congress puts Hollywood on trial when, in 1947, the House Un-American Activities Committee (HUAC) opens hearings on alleged Communist infiltration of the motion picture industry. The mood of the country has changed dramatically since our wartime alliance with the Soviet Union. Now, the Soviets seem intent on expansion in Europe and, it is darkly rumored, are undermining the United States. Strikes and spy scandals, Mao's victory in China and later the Korean War, fan paranoia. Hollywood, with its hold on the hearts and minds of Americans and its influence abroad is a convenient scapegoat for domestic unrest. Thunders Mississippi Congressman John Rankin: "(Hollywood is) the greatest hotbed of subversive activity in the U.S."

During the thirties, some writers flirted with Communism or joined the party to express their hatred of fascism in Europe and injustice at home. Some came to Hollywood, intent on using motion pictures as a sounding board. They were frustrated by the studio system, in which scripts were constantly rewritten and carefully scrutinized by the front office to eliminate any hint of controversy. Zanuck's involvement with *The Grapes of Wrath* and Goldwyn's on *The Best Years of Our Lives* demonstrate how fine was the net.

However, many in the industry consider business more important than people's private beliefs. Shortly before the HUAC hearings, Harry Cohn is urged to fire John Howard Lawson, a noted activist, who is currently scripting *Counter-Attack.* Cohn refuses: "I ain't going to louse up a picture that's going to do three million two domestic!"

In October, 1947, 19 witnesses are subpoenaed. Eric Johnston, Will Hays' successor as President of the Motion Picture Association of America, reassures their defense lawyers: "Tell the boys not to worry. There'll never be a blacklist. We're not going to go totalitarian to please this Committee. As long as I live, I will never be a party to anything as un-American as a blacklist."

Ten of the witnesses—producer-director Herbert Biberman, director Edward Dmytryk, producer-writer Adrian Scott, and screenwriters Alvah Bessie, Lester Cole, Ring Lardner Jr., John Howard Lawson, Albert Maltz, Samuel Ornitz and Dalton Trumbo—plead their First Amendment rights of free speech, and refuse to divulge, "whether you are now or have ever been a member of the Communist Party." They are cited for contempt of Congress, and are later tried and sentenced to a year in jail.

Meeting at the Waldorf-Astoria in New York, industry leaders agree to dismiss the "Unfriendly Ten" witnesses and discharge other suspected Communists or fellow-travellers. A blacklist is circulated which also covers radio and television and is greatly enlarged by subsequent Congressional hearings and by the denunciations of notorious red-baiters. The burden of proof is placed on the accused. Careers are destroyed and the fresh ideas that the industry badly needs are curtailed in a climate of fear. Not until the end of the fifties is the effect finally alleviated.

About 50 low-budget anti-Communist films are produced; they are as sparsely attended as were the few pro-Soviet films of the War era. More popular are the science-fiction pictures whose themes betray our anxieties about subversion and a nuclear holocaust. They show creatures from other worlds taking over our minds, and monsters lumbering in from the Mojave or rising from 20,000 fathoms to stomp on our cities. In the original *Invasion of the Bodysnatchers*, the hero reflects: "Only when we have to fight to stay human do we realize how precious our humanity is."

Years before television becomes a major diversion, theater-going begins to drop from its 1946 peak. Then, as now, it is likely that the biggest factor is the lack of quality movies. The captive audience of the war years has lulled Hollywood into a state of complacency. Another factor is

ca. 1949 The famous
Schwab's Drug Store, at
Sunset Boulevard and Cres-
cent Heights in Hollywood.
Many stars credited their
careers to having been
"discovered" here; however,
it really was a centralized
meeting location for
writers, actors and agents.

A tribute from
Century Plaza Hotel
and Tower

*ca. 1950   As the television
industry emerges, it centers
itself as close as possible to
the motion picture industry's
legendary Hollywood and
Vine. Here, NBC Television
and Radio, just two blocks
south, at the corner of
Sunset and Vine, is located
on the former site of
Famous Players Lasky-
Paramount Studios. Across
the street, the American
Broadcasting Company.*

*1952   A laughing
cameraman, a sympathetic
director, Howard Hawks,
and two nervous actors on
roller skates. Cary Grant,
Marilyn Monroe filming
"Monkey Business" for
20th Century Fox.*

A tribute from
Rococo

1952 Roy Rogers and Trigger gave one of Bob Hope's best films, "Son of Paleface" with Jane Russell, an unusual satirical punch. A scene where Hope and Trigger share the same bed, is an unheralded comedy classic.

1953 Makeup artist Allan Snyder puts finishing touches on redhaired Rhonda Fleming as she prepares to go before the 3-D cameras in the 20th Century Fox production of "Inferno," co-starring Robert Ryan and William Lundigan.

A tribute from
Christi Harris/ The Salon
Hugh York & Assoc.

*1953   William Holden
doesn't seem to be bothered
by the heat in Death Valley
during the filming of MGM's
"Escape from Fort Bravo."*

1953 The Hollywood premier, at Grauman's Chinese Theatre, of the first film made on an anamorphic or wide screen cinemascope process. Several anamorphic processes had been patented since 1898, but in the early fifties, when Hollywood was searching for a counter to the threat of television, 20th Century Fox took an option on the invention and named it CinemaScope.

A tribute from
The Seagram Classics
Wine Company

1954 Marlon Brando does his own makeup while on location filming "On the Waterfront."

1954   A rare behind the scenes look at the CBS set of "The Honeymooners" with Jackie Gleason and Art Carney.

A tribute from
Eastman Kodak Company,
Motion Picture and Audio-
visual Products Division/
Western Region

*ca. 1954   Jack Webb
directed and starred in the
feature film version of
"Dragnet."*

1955 On the set of "The Long Gray Line" at West Point. John Wayne visits his son, Patrick, a cadet in the film, which starred Tyrone Power (rear) and was directed by John Ford (center) for Columbia Pictures.

1955 Grace Kelly, portraying a beautiful princess in MGM's "The Swan," discusses the script with co-star Alec Guinness before a scene rehearsal.

1955   Few modern actors had such a profound affect upon young audiences as did James Dean. With only three feature films to his credit, he was killed shortly after this picture was taken.

A tribute from
Legacy/Cameron Hall

*ca. 1955   Walt Disney was
especially fond of railroads,
seen here with a real steam
locomotive in the backyard of
his home. It was modeled
after the larger version, a
featured attraction at the
just-opened Disneyland.*

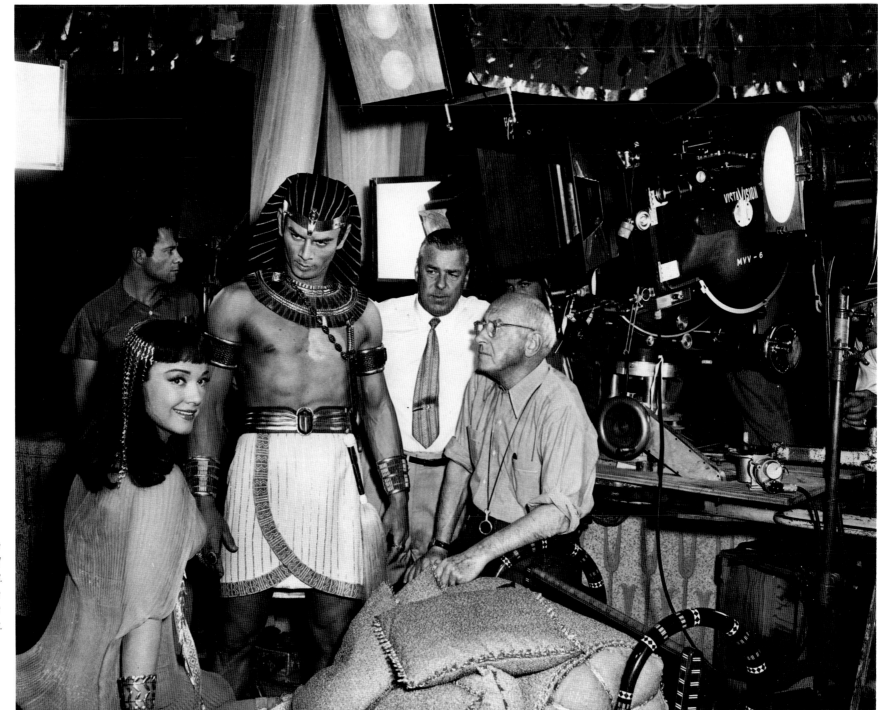

1956 Anne Baxter is the center of attraction for Yul Brynner and Cecil B. DeMille on the set of "The Ten Commandments" at Paramount.

A tribute from
Writers Guild of America
West

1957   Henry Fonda, during rehearsals of "Twelve Angry Men," in which Sidney Lumet debuted as a director, and Henry Fonda as a producer.

8

The Eighth Decade 1957-1967

By the early sixties, Hollywood is on its way to becoming a ghost town. *Life* sends writer Budd Schulberg, son of a former head of Paramount Pictures, to do a story on the industry. He finds that everyone he wants to meet is back in New York or abroad: "Where was Hollywood? How could I write about it? I couldn't even find it," he complains.

Moviemakers begin drifting away in the early fifties. In an ironic reversal of Hollywood's role as a haven for the oppressed, American writers and directors emigrate to Europe and Mexico as refugees from McCarthyism. To fill the CinemaScope and VistaVision screens, and to satisfy the renewed public appetite for biblical epics, there is a need for thousands of affordably-priced extras. Spain and Yugoslavia hire out their armies to ride across empty plains; Rome has the craftsmen who can recreate the temples and palaces of the ancient world. London has empty stages and a reservoir of underemployed talent. Sam Bronston builds huge studios near Madrid, and produces *El Cid* and *King of Kings.* Sam Spiegel ventures further—to Thailand for *The Bridge on the River Kwai,* and to the Jordanian desert for *Lawrence of Arabia.*

The center of the action is Cinecittà on the outskirts of Rome, Europe's largest studio. The first feature-length *Ben Hur* began shooting in Italy in the mid-twenties and the venture proved catastrophic. Now things are better organized and MGM's remake of *Ben Hur* is the top-grossing picture of 1959. Less fortunate is Twentieth Century Fox, which began its production of *Cleopatra* in London, is rained out, and switches to Rome.

Joseph Mankiewicz takes over from Rouben Mamoulian as director, the finest talent is poured in, but the $44 million blockbuster loses money even though it is the year's top-grossing picture. A real estate deal rescues the studio: Twentieth Century Fox develops its back lot as Century City.

Runaway production is a lethal blow to much of Hollywood, but for a decade it proves an irresistible lure. Foreign governments offer subsidies; producers can draw on blocked earnings; stars benefit from lower taxes. Above all, there are novel faces and locations to exploit, and creative freedom for artists and producers alike.

As motion picture production declines, and only television keeps the stages lit, the studio system crumbles. Contracts are dropped; talent is hired on a picture-by-picture basis. In the early fifties, Jimmy Stewart exchanged a part of his salary for profit participation. Now, all the top actors become free agents, able to charge what the market will bear; some—like Marlon Brando, Kirk Douglas, Burt Lancaster and John Wayne—form their own production companies. Agents become the new moguls, assembling packages, and even taking control of studios.

The physical structure of the studio changes. Location shooting and rising land values doom the back lot and the studio ranch; all but a few are sold to real estate developers. To save on overhead and to make room for the offices of independent producers, studios shut down the craft departments that were an essential part of the dream factory. Wardrobe and art departments are cut back, and props are sold—to be rented back when needed.

The old order changes. Harry Cohn, co-founder and life-long head of Columbia Pictures, dies in harness, as does Walt Disney. Louis B. Mayer, dethroned from MGM, dies in 1957 after trying and failing to make a comeback. Jack Warner sells piece meal to Seven Arts, the company he helped found. Gulf and Western buys Paramount Pictures. Later, Transamerica Corporation acquires United Artists. MCA, the leading talent agency, takes control of Universal and under the vigorous leadership of Jules Stein and Lew Wasserman, take it into the major leagues.

It is the end of an era when, in 1960, Clark Gable dies. Nicknamed "The King" during his heyday in the thirties, he was the actor whom Selznick had to have as Rhett Butler, no matter how high the price. But the actor who began his career as an extra in the twenties had few expectations. "Definitely, there was no future for me in Hollywood," he recalled. "I was no Valentino or Gilbert. I was somewhat of a roughneck." He tested for Warner Bros., but was dismissed by Darryl Zanuck: "His ears are too big. He looks like an ape." Which is exactly why he succeeded during the Depression, when his hulking frame and outspoken manner made him a working man's hero.

1960 Producer, director, actor John Wayne on the set of United Artists' "The Alamo," shot on location in Texas. The film marked Wayne's first directing effort.

A tribute from
Danny Thomas
Productions

*1960   A script conference
on "Make Room for Daddy."
Danny Thomas (center) co-
star Marjorie Lord (second
from right) and producer
Sheldon Leonard (standing)
at Desilu Studios.*

177

*1962   Jack Lemmon, Lee
Remick and Blake Edwards
(seated) with the camera
crew during the filming of
"Days of Wine and Roses".*

K

S

A tribute from
Atticus Corporation

1962   Gregory Peck won an Academy Award for his performance in "To Kill a Mockingbird," Horton Foote also won an Oscar for his screenplay of Harper Lee's novel.

*1964   CBS Television
reporter, Mike Wallace,
demonstrates the newest
technology in live coverage,
a 6½ lb. wireless camera.*

A tribute from
Michael Landon Productions

ca 1964   The cast of
"Bonanza." Left to right:
Pernell Roberts, Michael
Landon, Lorne Greene,
Dan Blocker. One of the
longest running early television series. Its first telecast
was September 12, 1959. Its
last was January 16, 1973.

1970 Ryan O'Neal and Ali MacGraw with director Arthur Hiller during the production of "Love Story," Eric Segal's story of star-crossed lovers that became a box-office hit.

1971   Warren Beatty and director Robert Altman flank cinematographer Vilmos Zsigmond during the shooting of "McCabe and Mrs. Miller" in British Columbia.

1976 Director Peter Bogdanovich with Ryan O'Neal and Burt Reynolds who star in "Nickelodeon," a fond evocation of the making of slapstick silent comedies.

A tribute from
Polaroid Corporation

1976   Robert de Niro with director Martin Scorsese, who also plays a cameo role in "Taxi Driver." Shot in the steamy heat of a New York summer, the picture combines harrowing realism with an operatic intensity.

ON RADIO CALL

OFF 3S96 DUTY

1977   Burt Reynolds starred in "Smokey and the Bandit," a good-humored caper shot on the back roads of the South.

A tribute from
Dana and "Cubby" Broccoli

*1977 Albert "Cubby"
Broccoli on the set for "The
Spy Who Loved Me," one of
a 25-year succession of
James Bond adventures he
has produced.*

10

The Tenth Decade 1977-1987

It is the best and worst of times in Hollywood. Never have motion pictures been more profitable, seldom has there been greater uncertainty about how to move forward. The industry seems destined to repeat its successes and its failures, over and again. The first James Bond picture was released in 1962; the nineteenth is due in 1987. Half the top-grossing pictures in a single year are likely to be sequels, and many are derivatives of the most recent blockbuster—be it a teenage comedy, macho fantasy or demolition derby. But whenever the Cassandras begin writing obituaries, along comes a rare treat: an independent production that breaks all the rules; a studio release that reshuffles old elements to recall past glories.

No star shines more brightly than special effects in the first half of this decade. The *Star Wars* trilogy fulfills the promise of Kubrick's *2001— A Space Odyssey.* It has an uncertain beginning. Only Coppola's backing allowed George Lucas to direct *American Graffiti* the way he wanted. Made for $750,000 it grosses over $70 million. Before its release, Twentieth Century Fox commissions the *Star Wars* script from Lucas for a mere $15,000. It takes him three years, and he has a hard time securing $8.5 million for the production, which lasts another two years. When the Fox executives see the finished picture they nervously try to spread the risk by selling a half-interest to Universal. The rest is history.

Star Wars is a phenomenon, cheered by the young audience, which returns over and again, as though for a religious experience. The lines wind around the block, day and night, for months. The trilogy has already generated a half billion dollars in film rentals, and a fortune in related merchandise. It gives George Lucas, who shifts from directing to

producing after the first of the three pictures, an unprecedented degree of independence, which he uses to create his own film colony in Marin County.

By comparison with later productions, the first *Star Wars* is made on a tight budget, and to achieve its multiplicity of innovative effects, an army of young creative talent is assembled. Two of its inventors, Richard Edlund and John Dykstra, establish their own special effects houses, Boss Film and Apogee, in addition to the original Industrial Light and Magic, to work on what now becomes a flood of space operas and special effects extravaganzas. Steven Spielberg's *Close Encounters of the Third Kind*, is made concurrently with *Star Wars*; later, he creates *E.T.—the Extra-Terrestrial,* a fantasy for children of all ages and the reigning box-office champion. Along the way are four episodes of *Star Trek,* three of *Superman,* two of *Alien,* and one of *Ghostbusters,* with a sequel on its way.

If space is the preferred location for the most profitable of current motion pictures, New York tops the list of terrestial settings. Increasingly, the Big Apple lures back the industry it lost to Hollywood in the 1910s. A growing number of directors and writers, actors and cameramen make it their base: Woody Allen and Sidney Lumet, Martin Scorsese and Paul Mazursky, William Goldman and Gordon Willis, Dustin Hoffman and Robert de Niro, to name a few. The Astoria Studios, former home of Paramount Pictures, are restored and rented out; new stages are added. But it is the streets of New York that have the greatest appeal: the energy and ethnic diversity of America's largest city.

Woody Allen defies all the rules of Hollywood, making a succession of uncompromisingly personal pictures, covering his modest budgets, winning critical plaudits and delighting audiences. He depicts a New York that's as idyllic as an MGM set of the forties, a world without graffiti or muggers, in which lovers can watch the dawn come up over the East River. Allen gets away with these fictions by infusing his pictures with comic invention, a wonderful interplay of character and a mastery of the medium.

By contrast, the New York pictures of Scorsese and Lumet are corrosive. They depict a city and characters on overload, where survival is a constant challenge, and death can be as close as the next doorway. This is why they are made on location, and why other moviemakers are ranging the country in search of new faces and flavors. Immigrant directors, accustomed to traveling light, reveal an America that the studios seldom showed. In the forties, Jean Renoir had to beg Darryl Zanuck for permission to shoot *Swamp Water* on location in Georgia. Today's filmmakers have no need to ask.

French director Louis Malle is a resident of New York, but he finds his creative challenge in unexpected places. *Atlantic City,* a drama of the old giving way to the new, is underlined by the city's transition from family

*1980   Rock Hudson plays
a Hollywood director in
"The Mirror Crack'd," an
adaptation of an Agatha
Christie murder mystery.*

1980 Colin Higgins con-
fers with Lily Tomlin, Dolly
Parton and Jane Fonda on
the set of "Nine to Five," a
breezy comedy that launched
a successful television series.

1982   Director Sydney Pollack plays agent to Dustin Hoffman in "Tootsie," one of that versatile actor's most challenging roles.

A tribute from
Columbia Pictures—a unit
of the Coca Cola Company

*1982 On location in India,
Richard Attenborough (left)
directs Ben Kingsley who
plays the title role in "Gandhi."*

1982 Sidney Lumet discusses a scene from "The Verdict" with Paul Newman, who plays a burnt-out Boston attorney fighting to save his career.

A tribute from
Warner Bros., Inc.

1988   Clint Eastwood meting out justice in "Sudden Impact." Dirty Harry and his trademark Magnum have drawn large audiences worldwide.

1984 Producer/director Ivan Reitman confers with Dan Ackroyd and Bill Murray during the making of "Ghostbusters."

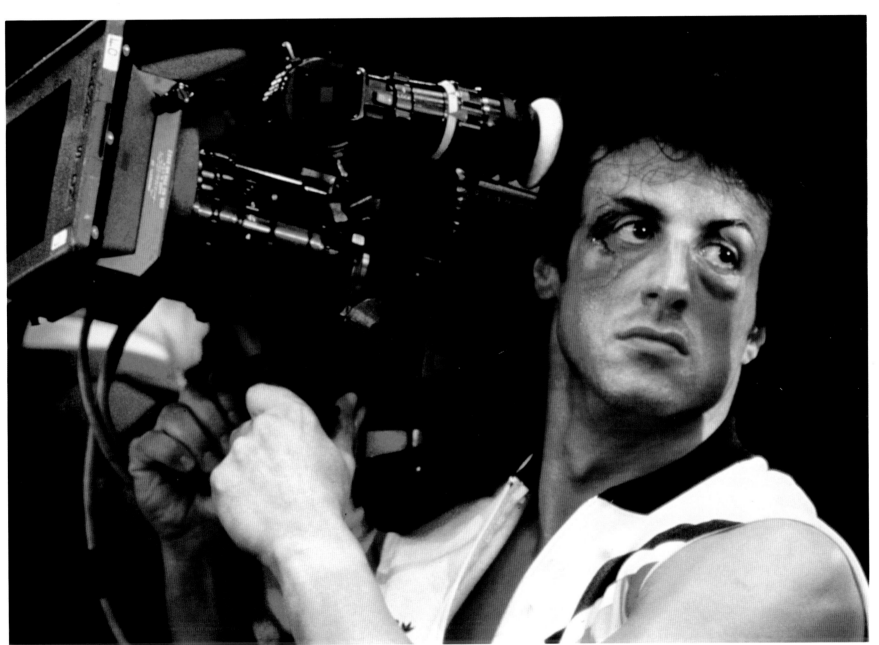

A tribute from
Sylvester Stallone and
Brigitte Nielsen

*1985   Sylvester Stallone on
the set of "Rocky IV," the
latest chapter in what may
be an ongoing saga of a
feisty underdog.*

1986 In "Poltergeist II," the Freeling family again finds itself terrorized by other world creatures. The MGM film, starring Jo Beth Williams and Craig T. Nelson, offers audiences state-of-the-art special effects.

A tribute from
Don Simpson/
Jerry Bruckheimer

1986   Tom Cruise (left) and Kelly McGillis join producers Don Simpson and Jerry Bruckheimer (right) on the set of "Top Gun," the year's top-grossing picture.

Acknowledgments

The Motion Picture and Television Fund wishes to express its appreciation to the following contributors to the publication:

ABC, Inc.
Amblin Entertainment
Robert Birchard
Bison Archives
Robert F. Blumofe
Eddie Brandt
CBS, Inc.
Stephen J. Cannell Productions
Stan Caidin
Bill Chapman
Columbia Pictures
Eastman Kodak Company
Karin Ginbey
Kim Gottlieb
Michael Hawks
Judie Hoyt
Ron and Betsy Isroelit
Jamie M. Jensen
Earl Lestz
Lorimar Telepictures
MCA/Universal Pictures Corporation
MGM/UA Entertainment Co.
MTM Productions
Roger L. Mayer
Movie Star News
Museum of Modern Art
NBC, Inc.
Dorine C. Nieuwenhuijs
Orion Pictures Corporation
Paramount Pictures Corporation
Gary Paster
RKO Pictures
Hal Roach Studios, Inc.
Jane Wooster Scott
Walter Seltzer
D.E. Slusser

The Bruce Torrence Collection
Turner Entertainment Co.
Twentieth Century Fox Film Corporation
Walt Disney Productions
Warner Bros. Inc.
Michael Webb
Boyd Willat
Mark Willoughby

Acknowledgments

The Motion Picture and Television Fund wishes to express its appreciation to the following contributors to the publication:

ABC, Inc.
Amblin Entertainment
Robert Birchard
Bison Archives
Robert F. Blumofe
Eddie Brandt
CBS, Inc.
Stephen J. Cannell Productions
Stan Caidin
Bill Chapman
Columbia Pictures
Eastman Kodak Company
Karin Ginbey
Kim Gottlieb
Michael Hawks
Judie Hoyt
Ron and Betsy Isroelit
Jamie M. Jensen
Earl Lestz
Lorimar Telepictures
MCA/Universal Pictures Corporation
MGM/UA Entertainment Co.
MTM Productions
Roger L. Mayer
Movie Star News
Museum of Modern Art
NBC, Inc.
Dorine C. Nieuwenhuijs
Orion Pictures Corporation
Paramount Pictures Corporation
Gary Paster
RKO Pictures
Hal Roach Studios, Inc.
Jane Wooster Scott
Walter Seltzer
D.E. Slusser

The Bruce Torrence Collection
Turner Entertainment Co.
Twentieth Century Fox Film Corporation
Walt Disney Productions
Warner Bros. Inc.
Michael Webb
Boyd Willat
Mark Willoughby

Photo Index